BEACON PRESS   BP 459 $2.9

Strategy

AND

Program

TWO ESSAYS TOWARD A NEW AMERICAN SOCIALISM

STAUGHTON LYND
GAR ALPEROVITZ

STRATEGY AND PROGRAM

STRATEGY
and PROGRAM
TWO ESSAYS TOWARD
A NEW AMERICAN
SOCIALISM

by
Staughton Lynd
Gar Alperovitz

BEACON PRESS • BOSTON

Library of Congress Cataloging in Publication Data

Lynd, Staughton.

    Strategy and program.
    Includes bibliographical references.
    1. Socialism in the United States—Addresses, essays, lectures. 2. Radicalism—United States—Addresses, essays, lectures. I. Alperovitz, Gar.
II. Title.

HX89.L94   335′.00973   72–6231

ISBN 0–8070–4382–6

ISBN 0–8070–4383–4 (pbk.)

For our children

Today any form of the concrete world, of human life, any transformation of the technical and natural environment is a possibility, and the locus of this possibility is historical.

—Herbert Marcuse,
"The End of Utopia," in *Five Lectures*

CONTENTS

INTRODUCTORY

We have chosen to publish this brief book because we believe it time to urge discussion of new approaches to the fundamental restructuring of American society. Working in different ways in different contexts we have found a number of our ideas converging, and although our areas of agreement are punctuated by difference, we feel that the sense of convergence (and the open acknowledgment of difference) may help stimulate further thought and action in the direction of our common purpose.

These essays confront arguments which have long been hurled at socialists, especially since the miscarriage of socialism in the Soviet Union. We believe, contrary to well-established Cold War stereotypes, that public ownership and democracy are not irreconcilable; that by moving toward public ownership and coordinated economic planning, popular participation in decision-making can be increased and power can be decentralized. And we believe that a movement seeking to create such a socialist and democratic society must prefigure that society by combining within itself the capacity to make and implement decisions on behalf of a mass membership and the freedom for individuals and small groups to take independent initiatives.

The first essay concerns political strategy. It stresses that radicals must both participate openly in other organizations and maintain a self-consciously independent stance; and it offers some ideas for ways to reconcile the values of participatory democracy with the need for co-ordination and leadership. Although the essay attempts to place our own society in the perspective of other capitalisms (and draws, for instance, on the work of European radicals like Ernest Mandel and André Gorz), it relies much more on the experience of the American Old and New Left, particularly in the 1930s and the postwar period: it urges an integration of that which is valuable in the traditions of both.

The second essay deals with radical program. It holds that it is important even in the Nixon era to begin a discussion of the society we would like to bring into existence as we move the brief two and a half decades towards the twenty-first century. Avowedly utopian, it rejects the illusion that serious programmatic development will come automatically (or magically) out of either history or "struggle," and instead affirms the need for self-conscious intellectual work on the nature of specific institutions which might achieve (and sustain) radical humanist values. It thus agrees with Julius Lester's judgment: "Yes, the system is breaking up, but it can only regroup around fascism if people are not presented with any other viable alternative. It is our responsibility to present that alternative. . . ."* The essay draws on socialist and anarchist theory, on foreign experience, on American history, and on contemporary community experiments for ideas which might contribute to a practical vision of the new society which might one day replace the old. It urges intensified efforts to develop the most promising experiments so as to begin to illustrate alternative principles in practice.

Although the two essays speak for themselves (and, we feel, complement each other) we would like to underscore a few areas of common emphasis. Aside from our shared desire to move beyond sterile "either/or" categories of debate (as in substitution of the concept "revolutionary reforms" for the false dichotomy "revolution" *or* "reform"), we have come by different routes to two practical judgments:

(1) We both believe it increasingly impor-

* "Aquarian Notebook," *Liberation*, June 1970, p. 40.

tant to define many local issues in terms of the *overall* community's interest. Hence, both essays stress the significance not only of traditional labor-related issues, but of community-wide concerns like taxes, pollution, education. In this connection such vehicles of community-wide activity as community unions, "parallel central labor unions," local labor parties, and community cooperatives and development corporations may take on a new significance.

(2) We both also have come to feel that a regional focus is important—both for political strategy and for long-term institutional development. There is need to decentralize the structures of the new society and the political and other efforts which seek to achieve it—and facing this need, we think, implies bringing together worker/community movements and institutions in larger geographic alliances. A politics of regionalism could—were it self-conscious—purposively aim to lay some of the long-term groundwork for a regionally restructured commonwealth.

The reader will undoubtedly note that the two essays differ in emphasis as to the role of counter-institutional complements to political strategy. The second essay stresses the concept of "prefiguration," urging the value of work now on practical beginning points of the institutions of a better society—even if present efforts can only go forward in a preliminary manner. It especially emphasizes the significance of community-controlled (and cooperative) economic endeavors—and of local institutions which hold capital in common on behalf of the entire community (especially those which use profit/surpluses directly to provide some community services). Institutions of this kind, which are emerging in many parts of the country, introduce the rough outlines of a different structural idea—and, despite their obvious present limitations, are one of the few practical ways of counterposing a collective economic principle to the widespread assumption that privately owned enterprise is inevitable. The essay does not affirm a simple "evolutionary" strategy, but argues, rather, that counter-institutions may play an important educative role in a more complex long-term political dialectic.

Viewed this way the emphasis of the second essay may be understood as an extension of the argument of the first that the Mississippi Freedom Democratic Party in the mid-sixties would have done well to combine practical politics with (for instance) the direct provision of community day-care services . . . and that an appropriate new strategy should do more in this direction. In such a strategy, it suggests, the

Left should ultimately aim to provide preliminary models of participatory institutions in all
ranges of life—both to help organizing by meeting needs, and to begin to suggest what is meant
by radical rhetoric in everyday terms. The first
essay, however, clearly stresses the more narrowly political aspects of strategy, subordinating
counter-institutional development to militant political organizing. Though we differ slightly as to
emphasis, we both believe that a new *combination* of politics and institution building is needed;
and also that the appropriate combination can
only develop out of further *praxis*—out of experience, out of trial and error, out of thought
and dialogue based on both.*

A word about our title, "Strategy and Program: Two Essays Toward a New American
Socialism." We have chosen it with some care.
We wish to make clear that our book is only a
small contribution to a large discussion—and
only in "two" areas; we have not addressed
many issues; we present only some thoughts on

---

* That our views are in closer agreement than the
two essays standing alone might suggest may also be
obvious from the *Addenda* following the *Notes* which
outline the context from which the second essay is
excerpted—and which (as urged in the first essay)
defines a number of specific areas in which a working
dialogue may be possible between the Left and other
groups.

"strategy" and on "program." The word "socialism" underscores our long-term hope; but we mean to imply that the word must be conceived differently from the way it has often been understood in the past, or in other countries; hence, our characterization that a socialism appropriate to our day and age must be both "new" and specifically "American" in form, style, and content.

We would like, finally, to say that we do not believe there are as yet answers to many of the basic questions we here address. Nor do we have illusions that there will be soon or easily. Answers will emerge only over the long haul, and only out of broadly based social processes. We offer our brief book in the spirit of tentativeness and exploration. We hope our ideas may be sufficiently specific to sharpen the debate, and sufficiently useful so that—in the course of continuing movement and dialogue—they may be improved upon, discarded, transcended.

May 1, 1972

S.L., Chicago, Illinois
G.A., Cambridge, Massachusetts

PROSPECTS
FOR THE NEW LEFT

BY STAUGHTON LYND

In the following pages I do not intend to pursue well-worn themes of controversy between the Old Left and the New. The truths to which the New Left testified seem to me as valid and important as they ever were, and moreover in need of frequent restatement. But unless we can move on to a more specific kind of discussion, drawing on what is best in the traditions of both Old Left and New Left, we are not going to build the mass socialist movement in the 1970s which I am convinced is possible.

Especially the need is to combine the best in both traditions practically, in terms useful to the organizer and active citizen. If most of the great debates between the Old and New Lefts can now be recognized as confrontations between two parts of a single larger truth (which it would be

sterile to continue endlessly, at least on so abstract a level of discourse), then now is the time
to talk again about more prosaic matters lower
down on the agenda. Exactly how and why did
the Old Left miss the opportunity to create a
labor party in the 1930s? What forms of leadership and decision-making do we want in a mass
radical movement? And what should be the role
of a Left wing within it?

No one paper or one person can do justice to
these questions. If the New Left is right about
anything, it is in believing that what each of us
should try to contribute to the common fund of
knowledge is his or her own experience. Perhaps, in reporting on my own work as historian
and as organizer, I can make a beginning.

THEORY AND ACTION

To begin with, while the New Left has yet
to produce an overall analysis, particular anal-
yses of particular problems have begun to
emerge. Mario Savio, one might say, described
the multiversity through his action; when he
asked students to throw their bodies on the gears
of a heartless machine he implied a critique
which at the time he could only formulate in
part. Since then a respectable mini-theory has
been formulated to explain the explosion of

youth. It seems that the rapid expansion of higher education is responsive to the new technology which calls for a university-educated "new working class." Conscription, for its part, serves not only to recruit a flexible supply of military manpower for imperialist wars but also to channel other young men into apprenticeship for the jobs which industry wants. Both in choosing a vocation and in choosing a Selective Service deferment the citizen is subject to "pressurized guidance" while believing himself to be free, exactly as in consuming objects he or she has been induced by advertising to desire. The principle of "repressive tolerance" applies not only to ostentatious permission for harmless demonstrations, but also to the more subtle and pervasive encouragement of pseudo-satisfaction of wants ("repressive desublimation").

All this goes some distance toward understanding the rebellion of the young, the white-collar proletarian, the student. Meantime Old Left theory also has been catching up with the new realities surrounding its old subject, the blue-collar worker. Ernest Mandel, especially, builds a bridge between the permanent war economy, the absence of a catastrophic depression, and the systemic tendency toward erosion of real wages through inflation. From this he goes on to the illuminating notion that because of state intervention in the economy strike action will increasingly pit the worker directly against the generalized employer, the state. Several New Left writers have noted that labor organizations are often most militant and more radical in a formative stage, before the signing of a contract with its dues check-off and no-strike pledge. Old Left theory may now be in a position to respond that the state's effort to restrict strike action will reproduce the situation which existed before collective bargaining was legitimized, and that the characteristics of that situation—tactical aggressiveness, rank-and-file participation in decision-making, concern for the oppression of all working men everywhere—will appear again.

Put together these two lines of argument, and the student and worker upheavals of May–June 1968 in France begin to make sense. Old and New Left theory join in comprehending the conjuncture of Old and New Left constituencies in practice. May we not, with these arguments and these great events before our eyes, begin to speak of an overcoming of the painful bifurcation between thought and action which has haunted post-war radicalism, of an end to silly discussion as to which of two equally essential constituencies is the "revolutionary vanguard"? Is there not a new possibility of students and workers, in their respective millions, patiently, carefully moving toward a political alliance in which each will speak in its own voice?

The promise of what happened in France contrasts sharply with the disintegration of the American New Left during the past few years. Underlying contradictions have not disappeared and (to quote Todd Gitlin from memory) society continues to make radicals more rapidly than the radical movement turns them off. Yet something clearly has gone wrong. Some say that SNCC and SDS had too little Marxist theory, others that they had too much. In any case one cannot continue to believe, as so many of us used to, that "the movement" was born under a lucky star which would make all its experiments cumulatively fruitful and extract from its experience just the kind and amount of theory and leadership that it required. That too was a kind of inevitabilism, which can no longer be afforded.

THE MISSED OPPORTUNITY OF THE 1930S

The New Left "blew the minds" of hundreds of thousands of persons, especially young persons, but has failed to create permanent organizations through which those who have been radicalized can express their new consciousness and begin to change the world. Campus-based, it has not reached the home-owning, union-belonging, over-thirty middle American, nor has it had much to offer to its own activists once they left the academic world and its environs. The New Left is strong on vision and weak on organization.

The Old Left had the opposite combination of strengths and weaknesses. It reached hundreds of thousands of ordinary citizens around issues of immediate self-interest and drew them together into stable organizations. But the process dramatically failed to transform the individuals who took part in it or to project a vision which would continue to be compelling after the immediate pinch of a self-interest issue was gone. Particularly in its uncritical support for World War II the Old Left lowered rather than raised consciousness, and left its members and fellow-travellers psychologically unprepared for the witchhunt that followed. (Consider, in contrast, the New Left's insubordination during the Vietnam War and the effect of that wartime resistance in creating what John McDermott calls a "popular resistance culture.") Only in recent years, as the scholarship of Chomsky, Kolko, and others has begun to describe World War II resistance movements which were inde-

pendent of all Great Powers and continually be-
trayed by all Great Powers, has the magnitude
of the Communist Party's failure in that period
become fully clear.

The most critical failure of the Old Left occurred not during World War II but in the
years preceding, 1929–1940. It is desperately
important to come to grips with that experience,
first, because it is the model of radical "mass
work" historically closest to us, and second,
because so much that is distinctive in the New
Left came about by reaction and overreaction to
what radicals did during those years. During
that decade a number of influential individuals
broke with the Old Left in a way that prefigured
the mass movement after 1956. Ignazio Silone's
novel *Bread and Wine,* for example, is a primer
of New Left attitudes: the rejection of dogma
and the return to elemental realities (bread,
wine, friendship); the celebration of action (one
man writing anti-fascist slogans on the wall in
the night); the shy courtship with religion (the
revolutionary disguised as a priest); the vision
of a movement as a band of comrades acting
out the future as if it were already here. In the
United States, during roughly the same period,
A. J. Muste broke away from Trotskyism, Bay-
ard Rustin left the Young Communist League,
Dave Dellinger rejected the contention of so-

cialist friends that prison meant political ir-
relevance and refused to register for the draft.
(Together, in 1957, the three founded *Liberation* magazine; later, Rustin organized the
civil-rights march on Washington for jobs and
freedom in 1963, and Muste and Dellinger the
great peace demonstrations of 1967.) Dwight
Macdonald, another ex-Trotskyist, put into
words a first synthesis of American New Leftism, in essays in *Politics* magazine cited by
Noam Chomsky 20 years later in his article,
"The Responsibility of Intellectuals."

Midway through the Thirties the Seventh
Congress of the Comintern adopted the "popular front" perspective, more or less adhered to
ever since, which gave Old Leftism the form in
which New Leftists rejected it. In America,
Hungary and Khrushchev's denunciation of
Stalin were probably less important in stimulat-
ing a New Left than the bland and manipulative
politics of the popular front. Many of the
founders of SDS were "red diaper babies," in
the loose sense that older relatives or friends of
the family, if not one's own parents, were in or
close to the Communist Party. Hence, although
too young to have experienced popular front
politics personally, the political style of popular front politics was very real to them (I

should say, to us) in the persons of the adults whom they knew best.

How to describe that politics and that style? The central assumption, of course, was that the enemy was fascism rather than capitalism, hence that the so-called liberal wing of the ruling class might be an ally. In the United States from 1932 to 1945 the liberal wing of the ruling class meant Franklin D. Roosevelt and the New Deal, just as in 1964 it meant Lyndon Johnson. The sentimentalizing of FDR, the New Deal, the Democratic Party, and the CIO bureaucracy by the Communist Party in the Thirties and Forties helps to explain the rage with which New Leftists attacked liberals and sought to unmask liberalism as an ideology which (in Carl Oglesby's words) "performs for the corporate state a function quite like what the Church once performed for the feudal state. It seeks to justify its burdens and protect it from change." The celebrated New Left revolt against authority was especially against paternalistic, indirect authority, against power—whether of parents, university presidents, Selective Service administrators, diplomats—cloaked in liberal words. In its concern to dissolve the alliance between radicalism and New Deal liberalism, the New Left tended to revert to the perspective of the Communist Party before the popular front, which held that the main enemy was not the reactionary Right but the liberal Center, not fascism but Social Democracy.

The attempt to build the widest possible coalition against fascism led to a habit of dissembling one's own beliefs. Little was said about socialism and much about democracy, and a certain deferential, ingratiating personal manner became characteristic which is still recognizable when radicals of several generations meet. The tendency was to rely not on one's own strength but on figures of authority whose charisma held the coalition together. I recall arguing as a ripe Marxist of fourteen against the "Browder line" which carried popular frontism to the ridiculous extremity of dissolving the Communist Party, declaring the class struggle at an end, supporting a no-strike pledge in industry to help the war effort, and looking forward to an era of international peace on the basis of unity among the Big Three. Apart from all these political particulars, what offended me (if I have not prettified this memory) was an abject dependence on persons in positions of power: Roosevelt in Washington, Earl Browder on Fourteenth Street in New York City.

A second personal experience was in the winter of 1948–1949 when, having dropped out of Harvard and journeyed across the country to

Oregon, I sat in the Portland Public Library reading the transcript of the Smith Act trials in *The New York Times*. Adrift as I was in my own life, it was peculiarly dismaying to read statements by Foster, Dennis, and the others which declared that Communists would defend their country in time of war, that Communism would come to the United States by parliamentary means, and so on. I contrasted not just the content but the tone of these statements with Eugene Debs' demeanor on trial for opposition to World War I. I felt ashamed for American radicalism. Much as I might sympathize with the Smith Act defendants, I could not respect them. (This dispraise of the Communist Party is not intended as backdoor argument for other variants of Old Leftism. In my experience Trotskyists outdid all others in furious haggling about resolutions which no one was in a position to implement.)

Such were the sorts of encounters with the older radicalism which led one premature New Leftist to look in new directions.

During the past year and a half I have had the opportunity to doublecheck my youthful impressions of the Old Left in long conversations with a number of Communists and Trotskyists in the Midwest who helped to organize the CIO. The pattern emerging from these conversations has, in turn, been checked with other New Left historians researching the same problem. Previously I was prepared to say: "at least the Old Left helped to organize the CIO." Now my impression is: "despite all that the Old Left did in helping to organize the CIO, the popular front line was more destructive in the labor movement than anywhere else."

Over and over again, it would appear, the Communist Party (a) failed to support the CIO rank and file in standing up against bureaucracy as embodied by the Murrays and Reuthers, and (b) threw its weight against the creation of a labor party. It was so in the Southern tenant farmers' union, according to Mark Naison. It was so in auto, not only according to Trotskyists with whom I have talked but according to a close co-worker of the Party in that industry, Wyndham Mortimer. In his autobiography Mortimer describes the role of the Communists at the crucial UAW convention in 1939, when R. J. Thomas was elected president rather than the more militant George Addes. Mortimer resisted pressure not only from Sidney Hillman and Philip Murray of the CIO, but also from a delegation of Communists which included Earl Browder, urging him to support R. J. Thomas.

And it was so in steel, according to several

memorable organizers. One man with whom I talked was fired for union activity in September 1936 and offered a job as an organizer for the Steel-Workers Organizing Committee. In his new role he suffered a series of rebuffs, not only from SWOC officers Van Bittner and Phil Murray but, to his dismay, from the Communists to whom he looked for help and guidance. They failed to support him in resisting the dismemberment of the local union he had built. When they were being purged in 1938–1939, he offered his support but the Communists preferred to be dismissed quietly. When the United Steelworkers of America was organized in the early Forties, he was the obvious candidate to oppose the international union's nominee for district director in the Chicago area. Bittner, Murray, and the Communist Party successively advised him not to run lest conflict be introduced into the just-created union. I had the impression speaking to him in the fall of 1970 that this man was still puzzled as to why the Left had let him down.

The argument of the Left was always labor unity. Why not resist a move by Bittner to subdivide and thereby decimate a strong independent local? Because of labor unity. Why not run an independent, rank-and-file candidate against the organization's choice for district director? Because of labor unity. Why not protest the patterning of the United Steelworkers of America constitution after the hierarchical design of the United Mine Workers? Because of labor unity. Why not fight against Murray's insistence that negotiations be centralized in Pittsburgh without even ratification of the contract by the rank and file? Because of labor unity. Why give up labor's time-honored weapon and agree to no local strikes or slowdowns? Because of labor unity. Just as the Communist Party supported Roosevelt in national politics and R. J. Thomas in the UAW, so in the Steelworkers it lined up with the conservative bureaucrat, Murray.

The rationale for the Communist Party's trade union work has been explicated in a recently published memoir, by the first editor of *The CIO News,* Len De Caux. "During the rise of the CIO," he writes,

American Communists followed the general policy of the Seventh World Congress (July-August 1935) of the Communist International. The 65 parties represented, including that of the United States, agreed that fascism and the war it threatened were the main danger. They urged unity of all anti-fascists in a broad, united or popular front. As applied to the labor movement, the policy was to build and strengthen trade unions, as a major bulwark against fascism. In place of the "united front from below," directed against social fascist" leaders of labor, the Communists were now eager to work with non-Red leaders for working-class solidarity.

"We advocate and consistently uphold the right of the trade unions to decide their policies for themselves," said George Dimitrov, the Comintern leader. "We are even prepared to forego the creation of Communist groups in the trade unions if that is necessary in the interests of trade union unity." United States Communists tried to follow this line in the CIO—to the point in 1939 of liquidating their system of union factions and shop papers.

De Caux confirms Mortimer's account of the 1939 UAW convention. ("Left to themselves, the delegates would likely have chosen a Mortimer-Addes slate. In this situation, some national Communist leaders urged the Left to set UAW unity, and wider CIO unity, ahead of personal and factional advantage and yield to Hillman and Murray. The UAW lefts reluctantly agreed—though some broke with the party over this issue.") And he adds the extraordinary story of Communist support for a Red-baiting resolution at the 1940 CIO convention.

How was Lewis, De Caux asks rhetorically, "to find a formula for convention unanimity on anti-communism, with Reds and anti-Reds diametrically opposed to each other?" He found it, continues De Caux, "in the weakness and/or opportunism of the Left."

A curious conglomeration of words was concocted. To odorize the whole with Lewisonian incense, it included a quote from Lewis' opening speech. Of those who attributed CIO policies to "communist philosophy, or Nazi philosophy, or any other philosophy," he had said that "they lie in their beard, and they lie in their bowels."

Coming from Lewis, who conceived most CIO policies himself, these words were both apt and true—particularly "or any other philosophy". . . .

The resolution then went on: "We neither accept or desire and we firmly reject consideration of any policies emanating from totalitarianism, dictatorships, and foreign ideologies such as Nazism, communism and fascism. They have no place in this great modern labor movement. The Congress of Industrial Organizations condemns the dictatorships and totalitarianism of Nazism, communism, and fascism as inimical to the welfare of labor, and destructive of our form of government."

To link communism with its capitalist extreme opposite under the jumble-word "totalitarianism" was just what the Hillman-Murray crowd and all rightists wanted. But how could the radical leaders of CIO's leftwing unions—some Communists themselves and all aided by Communists in building their unions—vote for this mishmash? The fact is that they did.

No doubt Communists acquiesced in centralization and anti-communism because, for the moment, they were still free to pass resolutions against fascism overseas. Once the practical freedom of local action had been surrendered, however, there could be no real opposition when the bureaucracy moved to purge its radicals. And in the meantime unaffiliated rank and filers were left out on the limb.

Here again the popular front practice of the Old Left was an important source for the attitudes of the New. Self-imprisoned within the limits of New Deal and CIO politics, the Left sought to salve its ideological conscience by passing resolutions. Little was done about these resolutions, but "one took a position," and that was felt to be significant. Verbal victories were substituted for action which would have split the organizations in which the Old Left worked. Understandably, and exaggeratedly, the New Left swept aside debating as a waste of time and asked everyone to put his body where his mouth was.

Was a different outcome possible in the Thirties? Could a labor party have been created?

All one can say is that it very nearly happened. The UAW convention in South Bend in April 1936 endorsed the creation of a National Farmer-Labor Party with the further instruction that "delegates to the forthcoming convention of the American Federation of Labor be instructed to introduce a resolution to this effect." John L. Lewis opposed the formation of a labor party, at least in 1936, but was radical enough to declare in a speech which launched the CIO drive in steel: "An economic dictatorship has . . . become firmly established in America, which at the present time is focusing its efforts upon retaining the old system of finance-capitalism, which was in operation before the depression, and thus preventing the attainment of political and industrial democracy by the people." It could have been the task of the Left to organize a third alternative to be available for a Lewis when he broke with Roosevelt in 1940. There would have been rank-and-file support. I found Lewis' 1936 speech in the papers of a steelworker, who, late in June 1936, wrote a "First draft of an analysis of the management's position on the CIO drive" in behalf of three thousand workers at a U.S. Steel plant in South Chicago. This remarkable document says in part:

> In France as we have all seen recently in the papers, a united working class government was placed in office a few weeks ago. Millions of workers have been on strikes in which no violence whatsoever occurred, because the government would not furnish police, arms or soldiers to bosses and their companies.

It concludes: "At the present moment the workers of the whole world are in a ferment, and the whole system of booms and depressions, profits for the few and hard labor and unemployment for the many, is showing signs of breaking down."

The Farmer-Labor Party in Minnesota suggests what might have happened nationwide. Its head, Floyd B. Olson, also opposed the creation of a third national party in 1936. Still he had said a year earlier, in an essay quoted by Howard Zinn, that talk about the impossibility of third parties was "sheer propaganda designed to discourage formation of a political party which will be representative of the aspirations of the masses." His own party, he went on, "talks about the cooperative commonwealth. There might be some accusation that the term is vague and nebulous, but it is nevertheless an attack on the fundamental concepts of the present system. . . . When one questions our system of wealth distribution, the line of thought must inevitably lead to conviction of the necessity of production for use as against production for private profit." This was the governor of Minnesota; and it is difficult to resist the conclusion that a Left outspoken for socialism while sensitive to its American constituency could have moved this man toward a radical third party.

Instead, the F-LP, which at its 1934 convention called for public ownership of all major corporations (including banks and factories), by 1938, under Communist influence, did not even call for public ownership of public utilities.

But this brings us to a deeper issue. Suppose the Communist Party in the Thirties had had the most correct of lines, abstractly capable of leading the American people toward a labor party and socialism. (I am using "labor party" in this discussion almost as a metaphor for a mass organization to the left of the New Deal and at least the more conservative CIO unions. To what extent such a formation should take part in elections, what concessions it should make to personalities like Lewis or Olson, what its relationship should be to trade unions, what attitude it should have to illegal direct action, are among many important problems not considered at this point, although some of them are discussed further on.) There would have remained a critical tangle of problems having to do with leadership and decision-making. Even if, for once, the Party had drawn the right number in the sweepstakes of Marxist prognostication, one wonders how many American workers and students would have accepted leadership for long from a movement the perspectives of which derived either from Moscow or from a handful of alleged theoreticians in New York City. The question of democracy is more than a question of taste. It is a question of the artificial or organic manner in which a movement grows, of whether the total experience of the movement is drawn on in the formulation of its decisions, of whether its contact with its own base is such that it speaks to persons not yet members standing just beyond that base, of whether decisions are final and binding or tentative and experimental, of whether there should be "organizers" distinct from participants, of whether the movement could continue were its leaders jailed. These questions take one back beyond Stalinism to the Leninist conception of a vanguard party bringing socialism to the workers from "the outside," and back beyond Leninism to the Marxist conception of political decision-making on the basis of "scientific" analysis by those with the leisure and training to undertake it.

Up to this point it has been argued:

That it is time to lay aside abstract debate between Old and New Lefts and to try to combine what was best in the political work of the 1960s with what was best in the political work of the 1930s;

That like the Old Left we must begin to build radical mass movements, but in a way that avoids the opportunism of the Communist Party in the popular front period.

It was also stressed, in passing, that a radical mass movement needs both white- and blue-collar workers as strong, independent components.

But none of this will happen unless the question of leadership and decision-making is resolved. Organization after organization in which New Leftists have worked has collapsed in a welter of charges and counter-charges of "elitism" on the one hand, "anarchism" on the other. Here, of course, both Old and New Left are touched on a most sensitive nerve. The redefinition of authority, including the authority of Old Left parents, is a short way of saying what the movement is all about. Understandably such a movement finds the creation of its own structure of authority traumatic. And as the New Left struggles with this Sisyphean labor, Old Left structures stand by ready to welcome tired young radicals into the fold with a murmured, "I told you so."

LEADERSHIP AND DECISION-MAKING
IN A RADICAL MASS MOVEMENT

I believe the New Left's attempt to find new forms of decision-making is significant and creative and in keeping with rational concepts of man and how he (or she) learns; I do not believe it should be dismissed as aimless irrational anti-authoritarianism. Once more, however, the point is not to defend the New Left's intention but to appraise in detail how that intention has misfired, and to propose alternatives.

Some necessary themes of this discussion are familiar to all. There is the matter of consensus and participatory democracy. There is the elitism which participatory democracy was meant to prevent but which in some ways it fostered. There is the question of caucuses, and the New Left's utter inability to deal with them. These themes can be dealt with briefly.

Why consensus prevailed in early meetings of the movement (including SNCC meetings, in the almost underground setting of the Southern movement) is something of an historical mystery. It may have had to do with the experimentalism everyone felt because social reality was so different from what anyone's theory had predicted. A journey is planned in one way if there is a road map. If there is no road map, if the country is strange and wild, and hills block off the view in all directions, if previous travellers have not returned or come back broken and dismayed, then the traveller is likely to move tentatively, stage by stage, surveying the landscape freshly as he tops each ridge. And meetings, under these circumstances, will naturally tend to a sharing of experiences already undergone rather than the abstract resolution of situations not yet encountered in practice.

But there was more to it than that. Consensus is the most natural and human way to make decisions. It is the way families and friends decide things. People who took part in the movements of the early Sixties will recall the fierce resistance to voting group after group displayed, simply because they had found something better. (Sometimes one took "straw votes" to get the sense of a meeting without calling it a decision.) As late as the fall of 1967, consensus was advocated in an article on draft resistance written by Dee Jacobsen of the SDS national office and growing out of discussions in which SDS veterans Vernon Grizzard, Paul Potter, John Maher, and Les Coleman each had a hand. Entitled "We've Got to Reach Our Own People" the article said in part:

> You are a serious resistance: don't vote on issues, discuss them until you can agree. All the pain of long meetings amounts to a group which knows itself well, holds together with a serious, human spirit, and any member of which can step into a role of responsibility if someone else leaves. Fight for that kind of group, because people will want

to join with it: there are not many things in this country like that. Stand by each other.

The weakness of consensus decision-making was simply that it worked well only in small groups. Once a group became large, and especially if those who composed it were heterogeneous in background and experience, consensus broke down. A longtime participant in the JOIN community union project in Chicago insists that voting was more democratic even in JOIN's meetings of two or three dozen persons, because the community people intimidated by the verbalism of student organizers felt free to cast ballots as they wished.

If we are talking about a mass movement then we are talking about representative government and voting. This doesn't mean (I shall argue) that small groups taking direct action after consensual discussion must disappear. On the contrary. But there has got to be a way for hundreds and thousands of people to set policy together regarding fundamental issues, and consensus is not it.

This conclusion should be easier to accept for Old New Leftists like myself because it is so clear by now that participatory democracy in large meetings in fact led to elitism. After the inconclusive discussion, a few people went back to the office and decided. This appears to be especially the case in movements which focus on periodic national events, like the peace movement, and was less a problem in early- and middle-period SDS, where the organization's action was the sum of what the local chapters did. Again to be personal for a moment, let me describe how I became a "peace movement leader." The week Johnson began bombing North Vietnam, in February 1965, Yale students who had worked with me in the Southern civil-rights movement asked me to speak at a university protest meeting. This led to an invitation (no doubt because an anti-government Yale professor was a man-bites-dog phenomenon) to chair a protest meeting at Carnegie Hall in New York. Then, on the eve of the SDS-sponsored protest march, in April 1965, the SDS national secretary (who already knew me) called me and asked that I chair that gathering too. In August several of us, who were besplattered with red paint as the Assembly of Unrepresented People approached the Capitol grounds, were prominently depicted in LIFE magazine. Finally, in September, A. J. Muste phoned to ask me to join "a few of us" in a small discussion prior to an anti-war movement conference. I had arrived at the center of peace movement decision-making by cooption rather than election, through a politics of friendship, and a search for leaders by the media. When, in December of that year, *The New York Times* informed me that I was a "peace movement leader," the process was complete. I submit that this is a profoundly undemocratic way for a movement to select leaders and make top-level decisions.

The New Left would probably have found non-consensual forms for somewhat-less-participatory decision-making had it not been invaded by Old Left caucuses. A first instance occurred when, after April 1965, SDS failed to give continuing leadership to the student anti-war movement. Moving into the vacuum, Communist Party members and sympathizers helped to create a National Coordinating Committee to End the War in Vietnam, with themselves in key roles at its national headquarters. Trotskyists responded by a disciplined attempt at take-over at the NCCEWV's first national convention. By the end of the convention a new national organization was being launched in a locked hotel room, the majority of delegates from grass-roots, *ad hoc* anti-war committees were bewildered and disgusted, and one more organizational effort was in a shambles.

In 1966 the Progressive Labor Party dissolved its front group, the May 2nd Movement, and directed its youth to join SDS. The new atmosphere of hair-splitting doctrinal debate frustrated SDS members who were pushing the national organization to involve itself in draft resistance, and led to their going their separate way to form the Resistance. PLP had much to contribute, particularly in its emphasis on the blue-collar working class, but imbedded this contribution in a style of work so dogmatic and aggressive that the existing SDS leadership took on the manner of the PLP caucus in order to combat it. Overnight everyone became a Marxist, not because this conviction had grown organically from experience (indeed, just at this time SDS efforts at working-class organizing were being given up), but because quotations from Marxism-Leninism-Maoism had become counters of value in an internal struggle for power.

About caucuses, perhaps one should conclude something like the following: 1. Caucuses are inevitable in organizations which grow large or are made up of people with very different backgrounds or experiences; 2. Nevertheless, there are caucuses and caucuses, and an organization can best survive them if all concerned agree: a. that all caucus meetings should be open to anyone who wishes to attend; b. that when presenting a position agreed on by a caucus, caucus members should identify themselves as such in workshops and plenary sessions ("speaking as a member of the so-and-so caucus, I favor the following . . ."); 3. What is most important is a certain openness and humility which cannot be legislated. Caucuses I have worked in which practiced points A and B (such as the radical caucus in the American Historical Association) have tended to transform the larger organizations of which they were parts rather than to destroy them.

The caucus within a larger organization illustrates microcosmically the broader dilemma of the staff of organizers, or party of professional revolutionaries, within a mass movement. New Leftists objected to the Old Left's failure to make the government of the Soviet Union wither away. But we run into similar problems when we organize. A scenario widely accepted in the early New Left held that the successful staff is that which organizes itself out of existence; that is, which exits from the scene leaving behind it an organization which can continue on its own. We have rarely achieved this, however, and it is important to ask why.

New Left organizational concepts are far better suited to the staff (or to the affinity group, collective, or vanguard party) than to the organization. The staff is smaller and staff members have similar backgrounds and experiences, hence consensus may work well in a staff. The elitism characteristic of staffs which operate consensually is usually an earned elitism: the leader is a Bob Moses whose authority is tacitly recognized on the basis of observed personal achievement. Caucuses may exist for reasons of personal antagonism or political difference within the smallest staff, but such caucusing is informal and, however painful, less a built-in problem than in a large and heterogeneous structure. When everything has been said that should be said about male chauvinism and the absence of "criticism and self-criticism" in early New Left staff communities, they can be remembered without the aura of nightmare which attends all memories of late-period SDS.

However, precisely because there was considerable "fit" between staff existence and New Left rhetoric, New Leftists tended to remain in the staff womb and to postpone the creation of large, heterogeneous, in some ways more prosaic and less romantic, organizations run by others. Large organizations make imperfect communities. Large organizations probably have less capacity to anticipate the lineaments of a future society than the small staff group in which intellectual and physical labor can be combined, authority and rewards can be made equal, and the quality of life can be humanized, more readily. Sensing this, the New Left usually failed to give organizational birth at all, and so failed even to confront the problems of post-partem bureaucracy which the Old Left (in the Soviet Union and elsewhere) so dramatically muffed.

SNCC is a case in point. The Freedom Summer of 1964 left behind it the first off-campus mass organization the New Left had created, the Mississippi Freedom Democratic Party. For the first time it was possible to organize in Mississippi in relative safety. Every organizational instinct should have directed SNCC staff members toward turning the precinct and county MFDP structures which had been gerry-built for the national Democratic Convention into real entities, and running candidates, operating institutions (such as the day-care centers which came into being under other auspices), mounting local direct-action campaigns; in short, challenging the Mississippi power structure in particular places day-by-day. Instead, with a few exceptions SNCC organizers left the state. They were exhausted from three years of struggle and made uncomfortable by the presence of white volunteers for the Freedom Summer who stayed on. But another factor, I believe, was that the MFDP was made up of persons older, less radical, and more interested in immediate small gains than the SNCC organizers.

Similarly SDS passed by the opportunity of creating a national student union and the peace movement failed to capitalize organizationally on the broad support it had mobilized by, say, the fall of 1967.

We draw back on the brink of building mass organizations because we fear they will be Frankensteins. Observing what happened to the CIO unions built by Communists and socialists, to the community organizations built along similar lines by Saul Alinsky, and to most if not all societies in which socialists have come to power, we shrink from permitting our radical congregations to become bureaucratic, reformist, coopted churches.

In the dead days of the late Fifties this attitude could be justified by the argument: "There are only a few of us ready to act, anyway." No longer! In any profession, the handful of radicals who slunk from pillar to pillar of convention lobbies ten or even five years ago now find themselves spokesmen for a third, a half, a majority of their co-workers. Outside the white-collar world, working people cast protest votes for George Wallace or James Buckley because the Left gives them no alternative. If, in the Seventies, we fail to build mass organizations it will not be because we can't but because we don't want to.

The reasons for not wanting to are grave. Large organization does mean representative government, even if the organization does not engage in electoral politics, and all that we have said about the superficiality of voting, the danger of shuffling off responsibility on representatives, the tendency of representative systems to talk rather than act, the possibility electoral politics offers for being a part-time radical who casts an insurgent ballot after a submissive work day, all this remains as true as before. Large organization breeds bureaucracy, an internal specialization of labor, the institutionalization of the full-time organizer who now draws a salary from an organizational budget. Large organizations do tend toward coalition politics, both within and without the organization's structure, because in large organizations goals have a way of shrinking to specific "interests" which can be traded off, made into composite packages, and compromised. No one in the past has talked about these things more than I, and I am unrepentant in insisting on their importance.

Still, if we are serious about changing our own society and about our responsibilities to oppressed people elsewhere, do we have any choice? Can anyone really imagine the coming of a socialist America without the prior creation of peoples' organizations, institutions of dual power, a labor party (I'm still trying to postpone consideration of the *kind* of radical mass organization needed)? The vogue of guerrilla warfare circa 1967–1970 can be partly explained, I suspect, by the fact that it seemed to offer a way of being revolutionary without the tedium of talking to masses of one's fellow citizens. We should open our eyes. No more dogged coalition-builders exist than the cadre of the revolutionary movement in Vietnam. There was all the difference in the world between Che Guevara's experience as a guerrilla in Cuba, where as villages were liberated the transformation of their whole life began and Che himself set up temporary clinics, and his tragic account of not swimming in the sea of the Bolivian people: gathering villagers together half-forcibly to hear a hurried and abstract account of the revolution before the pursuing government troops forced him to leave, without new recruits. In the Russian Revolution of 1917 there was no attempt to take power until the Bolsheviks had won a majority in the soviets. What all these experiences have in common is the revolutionary's confidence that he speaks to the basic needs of the majority of his own people. Without this feeling of being un-alienated, at home, swimming in a supportive sea when among the common people of one's own society, Leftists, whether Old, New, or inter-mediate, are not going to bring about basic change; and with this feeling, I submit, the nat-ural first step is to begin to build forms of collective struggle which express it.

More concretely, the question is how to work creatively within a mass organization which is somewhat radical (which is why you are in it) but not as radical as you yourself are. The art of radicalizing reformist structures, including structures we have helped to create, requires relearning.

THE ROLE OF A LEFT IN A MASS ORGANIZATION

I have attempted to describe how the New Left finds itself suspended between small cadres or communal structures, on the one hand, and mass organizations on the other. Conscious of the need to build more broadly than the first, we yet have been unable to commit ourselves to the second. The Thirties bequeath models of lowest-common-denominator coalitions and of a Left boring from within and maneuvering behind the scenes in left-of-center mass organizations. Rather than do that, we have usually concluded, it is better to put together something small in which you can speak your whole mind and act without bureaucratic delay.

I want to argue now that such action committees belong within rather than outside of mass organizations. They are the kind of caucus which the New Left can create most naturally, and a far better kind of caucus, in my opinion, than groups thrown together on the occasion of election of officers.

Consider the trade-union movement. Old Leftists who remain in industry tend to define their objective as election to union office. Year after year, they patiently inch their way up the hierarchy of the local union, from assistant griever to griever, from secretary of the grievance committee to chairman of the grievance committee, and finally, if all goes well, to president of the local. This strategy has proved no more rewarding than that of national rank-and-file movements which replace McDonalds with Abels. Once elected, the radical president of a local has little power to affect nationally negotiated contracts. I know of one man, first president of a large CIO local in the Thirties, who was elected again in the Sixties after two decades of the dirtiest sort of Red-baiting. Unable to deliver on his campaign promises, he was defeated at the next election by an opponent who reprinted John's own platform and asked the voters how many of these changes had come about.

In my opinion, a better approach within the unions would be to go for the powers which the Left gave up to the union bureaucracy in the Thirties: the local right to strike and the shop-steward system. The first major CIO contracts, signed in March 1937 with General Motors and United States Steel, took away from the rank and file in those corporations the right to speak effectively through on-the-spot representatives and the right to act effectively through departmentmental and plant-wide strikes. In place of a shop steward for every 25 or 50 workers, authorized by contract to leave his job in order to take up a grievance with the foreman concerned, the GM contract limited the "shop committee" to nine workers per plant and the U.S. Steel contract restricted the "grievance committee" to ten workers per mill. This is the origin of the cumbersome grievance machinery which today compels an aggrieved worker not to take action, at the time, on the spot, but to fill out papers which may take years to process (academics enjoy a strictly analogous opportunity vis-à-vis their own company union, the American Association of University Professors).

Similarly, both these precedent-forming contracts forbade strike action initiated from below. Both provided for referral of problems to arbitration by an umpire as a last resort. The GM contract explicitly stated that strike action was forbidden "without the approval of the International officers of the Union." And the unions involved, the United Automobile Workers and the Steel Workers Organizing Committee, rigorously enforced these understandings. Today the worker who "wildcats" can expect to be dismissed with the assistance, indeed at the insistence, of the union.

So far as I can see, the best spot for a radical in a union is to hold low-level local office (as a griever, committeeman, or whatever) but at the same time to be active in grass-roots organizational forms outside the union structure. This might be simply an informal association of the workers in the department he represents as a griever, who could test the limits of their freedom of action under the contract. (For instance, the steel contract permits a worker to refuse to perform a job he considers unsafe. What if a department refused together?) Groupings outside the formal structure of the union need not be limited to the workplace, however. A group of workers battling pollution in a particular part of the factory can establish a direct relation to a community group fighting the same pollution as it affects persons on the outside. In fact, a community group can give workers some protection from the union bureaucracy. Rank-and-file caucuses in different plants may find it easier to explain to the international union their presence at the same meeting if they are able to point to an organization in the community which called them together.

An analogous situation, closer to the experience of persons in the movement of the Sixties, is the relation of draft-resistance groups to the larger peace movement. Draft resistance is the striking-at-a-local-level of anti-war work, the thing which one or a few people can do to force the issue, the equivalent of wildcatting in a factory. Yet, on the whole, draft resisters and the larger peace movement have defined themselves as mutually exclusive alternatives rather than as supplementary parts. In 1966, as indicated earlier, SDS members most concerned to build a draft-resistance movement broke away and organized separately. In April 1967, the National Mobilization Committee at first opposed draft-card burning as a part of its New York City demonstration, and in the end grudgingly agreed that resisters might do their thing at the assembly point for the demonstration (Sheep's Meadow) but before the "official" demonstration began. Resisters, for their part, were perpetually confronted with the question: What do I do after I burn or return my draft card? In retrospect, it is astonishing that the answer was so rarely: continue the speaking, marching, and other kinds of organizing which are also important parts of the peace movement. It is as if persons who made the leap to resistance, or "ultra-resistance" (destroying draft files), felt obliged to condemn the less risky activities they had gone beyond as unimportant.

As mass radical organizations develop in the Seventies, it seems to me the New Left can best operate through groups similar to shop committees or draft-resistance unions which, while keeping one foot within the circle of a larger organization, also insist on acting out their convictions. In this way we can both learn from the Old Left, in recognizing the necessity for mass organization, yet keep faith with the New Left's insight that the best way to communicate a position is by exemplifying it.

At present, organization is furthest developed in the constituency best represented in the movement: academics and ex-academics. The radical caucuses within the Modern Language Association and American Historical Association are also members of the New University Conference, a national organization of socialist teachers and graduate students. Each of these two caucuses is in a position to "take power" in its respective professional association. Their members also recognize, however, that the day-to-day problems which confront radicals on campus require unity among all radicals, regardless of professional discipline or status in the academic community. Hence, on a particular campus they will be more likely to act as NUC members than as members of one or another field. In an industrial community, by analogy, members of rank-and-file caucuses in a number of different plants and industries might combine in a "parallel, central labor union" to deal with problems like taxation which affect everyone in the community.

Sometimes we will enter existing large organizations like the MLA and AHA, or a CIO union. There will also be times when we ourselves build a large organization. In the latter case there are things that can be done in the organizational phase which will make it easier for rank-and-file action committees to function later on. We can avoid operating through the existing leadership of established organizations and seek out the offbeat teachers' local, the small but innovative independent union of oil workers, the emerging caucuses in the International Brotherhood of

Teamsters (to draw on my own experience in Gary), or, to go back to Bob Moses' work in Mississippi, give recognition to the state president of the NAACP but build especially on the embattled officers of local NAACP chapters. We can also anticipate the substantive issues which will tend to divide the mass organization, once it comes into being. If SNCC had done more to emphasize the limitations of winning the right to vote at the time it worked mainly on voter registration, the MFDP might have been more conscious of the need for economic as well as political power and less vulnerable to the Democratic Party. A useful rule of thumb, in my experience, is to avoid easy political targets—the notorious mayor, the corrupt machine boss—and keep the focus on corporations. Last but not least, of course, at all stages in the process there must be some radicals prepared to insist on their long-run goals and to take the consequences. Whether the mass organization is prepared to defend them is an issue that must sooner or later be faced.

What is most important, in the context of the perspective I am urging, is to keep clearly in mind from the outset the model of a large organization which has the capacity to make decisions and take actions but which also allows freedom of action to its constituent small groups (committees, caucuses, branches, chapters, locals, affiliated organizations, soviets, or what have you). We need a CORE which will not condemn six members of its East River chapter for sitting down on the Triborough Bridge at rush hour to protest housing conditions in Harlem. We need an MFDP which will not repudiate young black civil-rights workers in McComb, Mississippi, where SNCC's activity in the state began, when they call for draft resistance. We want industrial unions which will defend local work stoppages unauthorized at higher levels. If we recreate a mass socialist party, we want it to be different from the pre-World War I Socialist Party which expelled the IWW.

Ultimately, we want mass organizations tolerant of smaller action groups within them because we want this kind of revolution and this kind of good society. The New Left has accurately intuited that an organization is likely to make a revolution in its own image. Democratic-centralist vanguard parties, for instance, can be expected to create revolutionary governments which will destroy local soviets. In advocating both representative decision-making in radical mass organizations, and small groups within them which act out new demands, risk expulsion, compel the large organizations to remember their original rhetoric, I am also saying that this is how a revolution should happen, and that this is what a new society should look like.

An aspect of the radical failure of nerve in this country since World War II is that few people dare to talk about how a transition to socialism might actually take place. In our hearts, most of us most of the time don't believe it can happen. I find that if I set aside all the old debates about direct action and electoral politics, and entertain the possibility that both kinds of action could be involved, then I can begin to imagine a realistic scenario. The transition to socialism in the United States, it now seems to me, would require both the election of a socialist government and mass civil disobedience, such as a general strike. Which of the two kinds of action predominates, and which comes first and just how they are related, seems to me less important than to accept the principle that both are needed. Perhaps the electoral transition would simply formalize a change which had already taken place in the shops and on the streets. Perhaps civil disobedience would be necessary to protect an elected socialist government and to make it do its job.

There are examples. May–June 1968 in France

is important again here, in that there was not only a general strike but very nearly the fall of a quasi-dictatorship. A general strike is said to have forestalled a fascist *putsch* in Germany in 1920. More to the point, in our own experience we have seen direct action cause a government to reverse the direction of its policy (or at least do so for a time, in some respects), cause one Presidential candidate to declare and another to withdraw, cause the government two years later to hasten the conclusion of the Cambodian invasion, and hopefully now, in 1972–1973, cause the government to decide against new escalation as it did in Spring 1968. It is true that we have not ended the war but it is also true that thus far we have set limits to its escalation. Imagine a bigger, broader movement, capable of impeding the off-campus industry of the country as well as the education industry; imagine dozens of candidates running for offices of every kind as declared socialists; imagine regional movements, in a number of metropolitan areas, which have won the respect of the electorate through gutsy action in behalf of obviously needed programs; imagine these things—none of which, singly, seems to me at all impossible—and one begins to envision a transition which might really happen.

The first step in this direction, it appears to

me, is not a political party (at least not a national political party) but the building and rebuilding of regional movements. The "parallel central labor union" or "community union"—which is exactly what the soviets of St. Petersburg and Moscow were—is a more useful model than the party, vanguard or electoral. It is a place to which particular groups of workers can bring problems which need broad support outside a single workplace, such as pollution and taxation problems; but also an organizational form which, by definition, tends to address itself to the concerns of working people in general. Its members should not be limited to representatives of groups of workers, but should include community representatives, as it were, grievance committeemen from neighborhoods. ("Workers" and "community" are not two groups of people, but the same people in their different roles of employees and residents of the community. A single person might vote for a delegate from his local union or rank-and-file caucus and also vote for, or be, a delegate from a parents' group, a conservation club, a writers' workshop, and so on.) Its characteristic form of action, as was the case with the soviets, will be direct action of one kind or another: strikes, boycotts, and the like. But this should not exclude the intelligent use of such political forms as administrative hearings; nor should it exclude discriminating participation in electoral campaigns, after the organization is solidly in being. There are many more kinds of election than for alderman, mayor or congressman, and these others—for union office, school-board office, and what-have-you— are probably the place to begin.

As such movements come into being and begin to grow, they (we) must be serious about being an alternative government. In a period of repression like the present, there is the temptation to be so preoccupied with survival and the defense of existing rights that, as in the Thirties, we let the question of socialism slip from view. To the contrary, the fact that the powers-that-be feel themselves obliged to attack what democracy exists can be used to win recruits for a vision of what a consistently democratic society would be: democracy, we must say again and again, can only survive as libertarian socialism, in which economic as well as political decision-makers are elected and the people take more part in decisions of every kind.

We are not planning a conspiracy and we should not hide as if we were. It is not our intention to manipulate people, to put something over on them through an innocent guise. We need to feel about ourselves and act consistently with the belief that we are trying to give substance to those aspirations toward a better life which people know they are being denied.

To be serious about being an alternative government we must be able to talk concretely about how a socialist society would deal with problems which oppress people now. Recognizing that much can only be resolved in the midst of experience, still we should begin to gather experience from other countries and spell out in specifics what a socialist approach to public health, a socialist system of education (if any), workers' control in particular industries under socialism, and the rest, might look like.

It may be said: there is no time. I think I feel the urgency, whether about nuclear war, genocide in Vietnam, or political repression, that others feel. I do not believe in bypassing present crises and organizing (in the old SDS phrase) for the seventh war from now. Yet I cannot see how a few friends pursuing hastily improvised programs by means of one or another single tactic can make a revolution. One thing urgency might lead us to do is to lay aside ancient movement quarrels and be humble enough to start fresh.

NOTES TOWARD
A PLURALIST
COMMONWEALTH

BY GAR ALPEROVITZ[*]

It is perhaps time—as Galbraith's loose assertion that the "Democratic Party must henceforth use the word socialism" should warn —that Americans interested in fundamental change begin to define much more precisely what they want.[**]

Where to begin a dialogue on long-term program? Historically, a major radical starting point has been socialism—conceived as social owner- ✓ ship of the means of production primarily through nationalization. Although the *ideal* of socialism involves the more encompassing values

---

[*] This essay and the Addenda to it are excerpted from my forthcoming *A Long Revolution*.

[**] John Kenneth Galbraith, *Who Needs the Democrats & What It Takes to Be Needed* (New York: Signet, 1970), p. 67.

of justice, equality, cooperation, democracy, and freedom, in practice it has often resulted in a dreary, authoritarian political-economy. Could the basic structural concept of common ownership of society's resources for the benefit of all ever be achieved, institutionally, in ways which fostered and sustained—rather than eroded and destroyed—a cooperative, democratic society?

My primary concern in these "Notes" on alternative program is with economic and social issues. There must obviously also be discussion of political institutions capable of preserving (and extending) positive elements which, though badly corroded, still inhere in aspects of the Western democratic traditions of freedom. . . . The central question at this point, however, is the structural organization of the economy. Achieve a valid solution, and various political alternatives may be possible (though by no means inevitable); without it, the power thrust of the economic institutions is likely to bypass whatever more narrowly political forms are created. . . .

STATE-SOCIALISM

Some of the main issues may be posed by reviewing the now familiar critique of statesocialism:

One major problem is that the concentration of both economic and political power in a centralized state produces what might be called an "economic-political complex," an institutional configuration not very appealing at a time when there is increasing awareness of, and concern over, the dangers of bureaucratic government. . . . The Soviet and East European experience attest to as much, and the dreary history of British nationalization (to say nothing of America's own recent Federal takeover of rail passenger transportation) is fair warning that the structural principle of nationalization is not in itself sufficient. . . .

A second problem is that classical state-socialism's dynamic tendency toward hierarchy and centralization reduces individual and social responsibility, and thereby destroys the basis both for freedom and for a practice and ethic of voluntary cooperation: to the extent decision-making is centralized to achieve the planned allocation of resources, alienation appears to increase. Individuals become ciphers in the calculus of the technocrats; hope of a humanism based on the equality of individuals working together fades. Arbitrary party directives, or (in some cases) the worst forms of market competition, then naturally become dominant modes of administration—for there must be some means of regulating the often inefficient, irrational, and irresponsible practices of bureaucracies set up to achieve "efficient," "rational," and "responsible" control of the economy.

State-socialism, thirdly, largely precludes maintenance of an underlying network of local power groupings rooted in control of independent resources—a political-economic substructure which might sustain a measure of restraint over central authorities. (The destruction of the *soviets* in Russia was a major turning point away from popular, democratic structures.) Effective democracy in most socialist societies is weak, particularly in relationship to economic issues. In instances of error or blatant injustice (as in Poland in late 1970) the citizen's recourse is to violent rebellion—now against precisely those agencies which were supposed to administer resources on the basis of new principles of equity!*

---

* Socialism's historic authoritarian forms are often attributed to the difficulties of capital accumulation in underdeveloped nations, to war and external threats, to the legacy of previous Czarist or Asian feudal traditions, to Stalin's personality, etc. Space does not permit an adequate discussion of these important issues. Suffice it to say at this point that while such factors are not to be discounted, the structure of classical state-socialism itself also has inherent tendencies away from participation and democracy, and toward hierarchy.

For such reasons—and also because of restrictions on political freedom, the absence of a sense of equitable community, and the drabness and sheer monotony of most existing socialist societies—it has become extremely difficult to imagine the Old Left objective of nationalization ever alone achieving many ideals—difficult to imagine especially for young radicals who affirm a new vision of personal fulfillment and who urge "let the people decide" in their own local environments! Centralized state-socialism as the centerpiece of radical program would make a mockery of such principles, especially in continent-spanning America which, by the end of the century, will encompass 300 million individuals.

In sum, although the concept of socialism involves a broad humanist vision, it has yet to be demonstrated how in advanced industrial settings the abstract ideals might be achieved and sustained *in practice*. While some form of social ownership of capital and the planned use of society's wealth may be necessary to deal adequately with many economic issues, the question remains precisely *what* form? We return to the basic issue: could society ever be organized equitably, cooperatively, humanely, so wealth benefited everyone—without generating a highly centralized, authoritarian system?

ALTERNATIVES TO CENTRALIZATION

A number of traditions have attempted to confront difficulties inherent in the centralizing tendencies of state-socialism; consideration of some of their alternatives suggests an initial approach to defining elements of a positive program:

It is helpful to acknowledge frankly at the very outset that some traditional conservatives (as opposed to rightist demagogues) have long been correct to argue that centralization of both economic and political power leaves the citizen virtually defenseless, without any *institutional* way to control major issues which affect his life. They have objected to state-socialism on the grounds that it destroys individual initiative, responsibility, and freedom—and have urged that privately held property (particularly that of the farmer or small capitalist entrepreneur) at least offers a man some independent ground to stand on in the fight against what they term "statism." Finally, most have held that the competitive market can work to make capitalists responsible to the needs of the community.

Some conservatives have also stressed the concept of "limits," especially limits to state power, and like some new radicals have emphasized the importance of voluntary participation and individual, personal responsibility. Karl Hess, Murray Rothbard, and Leonard Liggio, among others of the Libertarian Right, have recently begun to reassert these themes—as against old socialists, liberals, *and* more modern "statist" conservatives like William Buckley, Jr. The conservative sociologist Robert A. Nisbet argues additionally that voluntary associations should serve as intermediate units of community and power between the individual and the state.*

Few traditional conservatives or members of the Libertarian Right, however, have recognized the socialist argument that *private property* and the competitive market as sources of independence, power, and responsibility have led historically to other horrendous problems, including exploitation, inequality, ruthless competition, individual alienation, the destruction of community, expansionism, imperialism, war. . . .

A second alternative—also an attempt to organize economic power away from the centralized state—is represented by the Yugoslav argument for workers' self-management. Whereas private property (in principle if not in practice) implies decentralization of economic power to individuals, workers' self-management involves

* See especially Nisbet's *Community and Power* (original title, *Quest for Community,* 1953) (New York: Oxford University Press, 1962).

decentralization to the social and organizational unit of those who work in a firm. This alternative may even be thought of as a way to achieve the conservative anti-statist purpose—but to establish different, socially defined priorities over economic resources.

The Yugoslav model of decentralization raises a series of difficult problems: though the Yugoslavs proclaim themselves socialists and urge that the overall industrial system must benefit the entire society, the various workers' groups which actually have direct control of industrial resources are each inevitably only *one part* of society. And as many now see, there is no obvious reason why such (partial) groups will not develop special interests ("workers' capitalism") which run counter to the interests of the broader community.

Indeed, problems very much akin to those of a system based on private property have begun to develop in Yugoslavia. Overreliance on the market has not prevented inequality between communities, and has led to commercialism and exploitation. Both unemployment and inflation also plague Yugoslavia. An ethic of individual gain and profit has often taken precedence over the ideal of cooperation. Worker participation, in many instances, is more theory than practice. Meanwhile, as competitive tendencies emerge between various worker-controlled industries, side by side the need for some central coordination has produced other anomalies: the banks now control many nationwide investment decisions, severely reducing local economic power; the Yugoslav Communist party takes a direct and often arbitrary hand in both national and local decisions. In general, it has been extremely difficult for social units to develop a sense of reciprocal individual responsibility as the basis for an equitable community of mutual obligation.*

The Yugoslav model recalls the historic themes of both guild socialism and syndicalism. It is also closely related to the "participatory economy" alternative recently offered by Jaroslav Vanek, and the model of workers' participation proposed by Robert A. Dahl.** All alternatives of this kind, unfortunately, suffer from a major contradiction: it is difficult to see how a political-economy based primarily on the organization of groups by function could ever achieve a

* See below for discussion of other problems related to Yugoslav practices.

** See, for instance: Jaroslav Vanek, *The Participatory Economy* (Ithaca: Cornell University Press, 1971); *The General Theory of Labor-Managed Economics* (Ithaca: Cornell University Press, 1970); Robert A. Dahl, *After the Revolution?* (New Haven & London: Yale University Press, 1970); Kenneth Coates and Anthony Topham, *Industrial Democracy in Great Britain* (London: MacGibbon & Kee, 1968).

just society, since the various structural alternatives seem inherently to tend toward the self-aggrandizement of each functional group—*as against* the rest of the community.

The point may perhaps be most easily understood by imagining workers' control or ownership of the General Motors Corporation in America—an idea close to Dahl's alternative. It should be obvious that: (1) There is no reason to expect white male auto workers easily to admit more blacks, Puerto Ricans, or women into "their" industry when unemployment prevails; (2) No internal dynamic is likely to lead workers automatically or willingly to pay out "their" wages or surpluses to reduce pollution "their" factory chimney might pour onto the community *as a whole;* (3) Above all, the logic of the system militates against going out of "their" business when it becomes clear that the automobile-highway mode of transportation (rather than, say, mass transit)* is destructive of the community as a whole though perhaps profitable for "their" industry.

Dahl, for one, is aware of some of these shortcomings; he hopes through interest group representation that somehow an "optimum combination" of worker and general community interests

* Or, simply *less* transit—and more planned co-location of functions.

might perhaps be worked out. Clearly, were a socialist framework substituted for the capitalist market such problems might in part be alleviated. The Yugoslav experience (where both the commune and the nation have extensive powers), however, teaches that socialism does not automatically resolve either the market's difficulties or the root contradiction inherent in a context which structurally opposes the interests of workers and society as a whole.

Some basic distinctions must be confronted. First, while management by the people who work in a firm should be affirmed, the matter of emphasis is of cardinal importance; "workers' control" should be conceived in the broader context of, and subordinate to, the *entire community*. In order to break down divisions which pose one group against another and to achieve equity, accordingly, the social unit at the heart of any proposed new system should, so far as possible, *be inclusive of all the people*—minorities, the elderly, women, youth—not just the "workers" who have paid "jobs," and who at any one time normally number only some forty percent of the population and sixty percent of the adult citizenry.

A second, perhaps more difficult, point: the only social unit inclusive of *all* the people is one based on geographic contiguity. This, in the context of national geography, is the *general* socialist argument; the requirement of decentralization simply reduces its scale. In a territorially defined *local* community, a variety of functional groups must coexist, side by side. Day-to-day communication is possible (indeed, individuals are often members of more than one group); and long-term relationships can be developed. Conflicts must inevitably be mediated directly by people who have to live with the decisions they make. There are, of course, many issues which cannot be dealt with locally, but at least a social unit based on common location proceeds from the assumption of comprehensiveness, and this implies a decision-making context in which the question "How will a given policy affect *all* the community?" is more easily posed.

When small, territorially defined communities control capital or land socially (as, for instance, in the Israeli kibbutz or the Chinese commune), unlike either capitalism or socialism, there is no built-in contradiction between the interests of owners or beneficiaries of industry (capitalist *or* local workers) *as against the community as a whole*. The problem of "externalities," moreover, is in part "internalized" by the structure itself: since the community as a whole controls productive wealth, *it,* for instance, is in a position to decide rationally whether to pay the costs of eliminating the pollution its own industry causes for its own people. The entire community also may decide how to divide work equitably among all its citizens. . . . ·

Although small scale ownership of capital might resolve some problems it raises others: the likelihood that if workers owned General Motors they might attempt to exploit their position—or oppose changes in the nation's overall transportation system—illuminates a problem which a society based on cooperative communities would also face. So long as the social and economic security of *any* economic unit is not guaranteed, it is likely to function to protect (and, out of insecurity, *extend*) its own special, status quo interests—even when they run counter to the broader interests of the society. The only long-run answer to the basic expansionist tendency of all market systems is to establish some stable larger structural framework to sustain the smaller constituent elements of the political-economy. This poses the issue, of course, of the relative distribution of power between small units and large frameworks, and of precisely which functions can be decentralized and which cannot.

Some of the above questions may perhaps be explored most easily in the context of the alternative to centralization represented by the localized practice of cooperative community socialism in the Israeli kibbutz—an historically agricultural institution which is now rapidly becoming industrialized.* The many existing variations of the model suggest numerous alternative ways to make decisions involving not only workers' self-management but community (social) uses of both capital and surpluses. Some approaches have been successful, some obviously mistaken and wasteful. . . .

Within the best communities one major point deserves emphasis: individual responsibility—to act, to take initiative, to build cooperation voluntarily—is a necessary precondition of a community of mutual, reciprocal obligation, and, ultimately, the only real protection against bureaucracy. When the ethic of an equitable, inclusive community is achieved, the efficacy of true "moral incentives" is dramatically revealed: individuals are neither paid nor valued according to their "product," but simply because of their membership in the community. But there are huge problems even in the best settings, not the

---

* The kibbutzim demonstrate, incidentally, that small industrial units can be highly efficient—contrary to theorists who claim large scale is a technical necessity. The kibbutz movement has continued to grow in Israel, although the proportionate role of this sector has diminished as huge migrations have swelled the capitalist economy since 1948.

least of which is that small communities tend easily to become overbearing and ethnocentric. If they are to break out of conformity they must allow a range of free individual initiative—without waiting for majority approval. And they must find ways to achieve flexibility and openness to prevent provincialism and antagonism against outsiders or (all) "others". . . .

The kibbutzim as a group have experimented with confederation, an idea which begins with democratic decentralization as a first premise, and attempts to build a cooperative structure between small units yet remain responsible to them. The confederate framework in part—but only in part—also helps deal with the issue of economic insecurity and the self-aggrandizing expansionist logic of market systems. . . .

The kibbutz experience is of course not transferable directly to advanced industrial society. However, it is highly suggestive as an expression of a final major tradition which attacked centralization: anarchism—a philosophical tendency in which there has historically been a long-standing debate about socialism, about whether it is possible to have individual freedom *without* a framework of state ownership of wealth, about whether it is possible to have it *with* state ownership. The most hopeful attempts to resolve the issue center on abstract formulations like Noam

Chomsky's "libertarian socialism," but this idea has not been developed much beyond the level of generalization. Anarchist theory has always been aware of the danger of both a socialist "red bureaucracy" (in Bakunin's term) and *laisser faire* capitalism, but it has no fully developed program. . . .

One may raise objections to practical failings of the existing models or to theoretical aspects of the various traditions, but it is hard to disagree with the judgment that centralization through corporate capitalism, fascism, or state-socialism has destructive implications for local communities—for all the people, that is, except the managing elites (and for them, too, in more subtle, insidious ways). Accordingly, whether one accepts the conservative view that individuals must control capital, or the Yugoslav that workers must, or the radical Israeli or anarcho-communist view that "communities" smaller than the nation state must, we are compelled to come to terms with the general proposition that political power has in some way to be related to decentralized economic power, at least until the post-industrial era. . . .

A PLURALIST COMMONWEALTH?

To review and affirm *both* the socialist vision

and the decentralist ideal is to suggest that a basic problem of positive alternative program is how to define community economic institutions which are egalitarian and equitable in the traditional socialist sense of owning and controlling productive resources for the benefit of all, *but* which can prevent centralization of power, *and,* finally, which over time can permit new social relations capable of sustaining an ethic of individual responsibility and group cooperation upon which a larger vision must ultimately be based.

A major challenge of positive program, therefore, is to create "common-wealth" institutions which, through decentralization and cooperation, achieve new ways of organizing economic and political power so that the people (in the local sense of that word) really do have a chance to "decide"—and so that face-to-face relations establish values of central importance to the larger units of society as a whole. . . .

Small units are obviously only part of the answer. My own view is that it is necessary to (1) affirm the principle of collective ownership or control of capital (and democratically planned disposition of surplus), and (2) extend it, at least initially, to local communities, the sub-units of which are sufficiently small so that individuals can, in fact, learn cooperative relationships *in practice*. These, however, should be conceived only as elements of a larger solution—as the natural building blocks of a reconstructed nation of regional commonwealths.

The sketch of a long-term vision might begin with the neighborhood in the city and the county in the countryside (and pose as a research problem which industries—from shoe repair to steel refining—can usefully be decentralized and which cannot, and what scale—say, between 30,000 and 100,000—is appropriate for "communities."* Its longer thrust, however, is more complicated: in place of the streamlined socialist planned state which depends upon the assumption of power at the top, I would substitute an organic, diversified vision—a vision of thousands of small communities, each organized cooperatively, each working out its own priorities and methods, each generating broader economic criteria and placing political demands on the larger system out of this experience. The locality should be conceived as a basis for (not an alternative to) a larger framework of regional and national coordinating institutions.

In its local form, such a vision is obviously greatly supportive of the ideal of community proposed by Percival and Paul Goodman in their book *Communitas*.* More specifically, a

* With sub-units of still smaller scale. See below.

community which owned substantial industry cooperatively and used part of its surplus for its own social services would have important advantages: it could experiment, without waiting for bureaucratic decrees, with new schools, new training approaches, new self-initiated investments (including, perhaps, some small private firms). It could test various worker-management schemes. It would be free for a range of independent social decisions based upon independent control of some community economic resources. It could grapple directly with efforts to humanize technology. It could, through coordination and planning, reorganize the use of time, and also locate jobs, homes, schools so as to maximize community interaction and end the isolated prison aspects of all these presently segregated units of life experience.

Communities could work out in a thousand diverse localities a variety of new ways to reintegrate a community—to define productive roles for the elderly, for example, or to redefine the role of women in community. They could face squarely the problem of the "tyranny of the majority" (and the concomitant issues of minority rights, and individual privacy), and experi-

---

* See especially Scheme II. Percival and Paul Goodman, *Communitas* (Chicago: University of Chicago Press, 1947).

ment with new ways to guarantee individual and minority initiative. The anarchist demand for freedom could be faced in the context of a cooperative structure. The issue of legitimate leadership functions might be confronted rather than wished away; and various alternatives, including rotation, recall, apprenticing, etc., might be tested. Communities might even begin to regard themselves as communities—communes, if you like—in the equitable, cooperative, humane sense of that term.

In their larger functions communities would obviously have to work together, for both technological and economic reasons. Modern technology, in fact, permits great decentralization—and new modifications can produce even greater decentralization if that is a conscious objective. In cases where this is not possible or intolerably uneconomical (perhaps, for example, some forms of heavy industry, energy production, transportation) larger confederations of communities in a region or in the integrated unit of the nation state would be appropriate—as they would be for other forms of coordination as well.

The themes of the proposed alternative thus are indicated by the concepts of cooperative community and the Commonwealth of Regions. The program might best be termed "A Pluralist Commonwealth"—"Pluralist," to emphasize decentralization and diversity; "Commonwealth," to focus on the principle that wealth should cooperatively benefit all.

The vision, of course, is utopian, but perhaps in the positive sense of the word, it is a set of ideals to be discussed, a long-range forecast of ultimate objectives. Its purpose is not to blueprint the future but to help define areas for serious inquiry and experimentation, and to facilitate a serious dialogue about the relationship between present action and future consequences.

LEVELS OF COMMUNITY

"The crux of the problem," Kenneth Boulding observed in 1968, "is that we cannot have community unless we have an aggregate of people with some decision-making power. . . . It is easier for a relatively small unit to have some sense of community. . . ."* Although Boulding offered his argument in connection with management of traditional municipal services, in my opinion his point applies in many instances to economic matters as well—but it raises a host of very specific problems:

Could conflicts of interest within com-

* Kenneth E. Boulding, "The City as an Element in the International System," *Daedalus,* Fall 1968, p. 1118.

munities, for instance, be more rationally resolved by new cooperative principles of ownership without engendering *local* bureaucracies?

If each community were restructured so that it might engage its own development more directly, how, more specifically, might it establish a basis for cooperative trade between communities, and for control of larger industry?

How might large scale planning, investment, trade, economic balance, and ownership/control issues be wisely addressed?

There is no doubt that cooperative development proceeds best in communities sufficiently small so that social needs are self-evident. Voluntarism and self-help can achieve what centralized propaganda cannot—namely, engender group involvement, cooperative enthusiasm, spontaneity. This is a primary reason to emphasize small scale local structures *at the outset*— even if it may entail short term disadvantages. The hope is that thereafter, with the benefit of a real basis in some cooperative experience, it may be possible to transcend historical starting points in the longer development of a larger framework. . . .

A key question is how to prevent local centralization of power: individuals as well as small groups must obviously retain some power as opposed to the local collectivity as a whole. (And the organization of individuals and small groups *is* power—power to prevent bureaucratic domination, even in small settings.) One answer is self-conscious individual responsibility—and therefore another requirement is the achievement of local practices and relationships which build the experience of responsibility at the same time they constrain bureaucracy. This will require a further breakdown into smaller subgroupings organized both by function and neighborhood geography within communities. (A "city" might be understood as a confederation of smaller communities.)* Another answer might be to distribute "vouchers" to individuals so they could freely choose different forms of public services like education and medicine. Such a financial mechanism would permit substantial freedom of operation for a variety of semi-com-

---

* The Israeli kibbutz confederation, with units dispersed throughout the geographically compact *nation,* hints at how small neighborhood communities might conceivably agglomerate into a larger decentralized city when telescoped, conceptually, to more compact *local* sites. In many local units, incidentally, power has become so constrained, and so divorced from significant prestige and status, that it is difficult to find candidates willing to accept the responsibility and drudgery of some top positions.

petitive, nonprofit service institutions. ("Socialized surplus," "anarchist administration". . . .)*

The need for a larger scale framework becomes obvious when problems of market behavior are considered more closely: what if every community actually owned and controlled substantial industry?** Even if each used a share of surpluses for social purposes as democratically decided, even if each began to evolve the idea of planned economic and social development, even if its people began to develop social experiences and a new ethic of cooperation—there would still be competition in the larger unit of the region or nation. Community industry would vie with community industry, neighborhood versus neighborhood, county versus county, city

* This approach is already in use, obviously, in Medicare payments and in some transferable higher education scholarships. It will surely be extended for health care. "Tuition vouchers" for elementary education have been proposed by a diverse group ranging from Paul Goodman to Milton Friedman and Christopher Jencks; and an O.E.O. experiment may test a version in the near future. Housing "vouchers" are also now being tested. The "voucher" approach may perhaps be best understood as a "transition mechanism" (to facilitate the establishment of a variety of voluntary and community controlled institutions), rather than as a final solution to the problems of public bureaucracy.

** See below for a brief review of current, rapidly expanding community ownership efforts.

versus city. If communities were simply to float in the rough sea of an unrestricted market, the model would likely end in "community capitalism," trade wars, expansionism, and the self-aggrandizing exploitation of one community by another. As in modern capitalism, there also would likely be both unemployment and inflation, ruthless competition and oligopoly, etc. (And within communities one result would be a tendency to exploit wage employees, as some kibbutzim exploit Arabs. . . .)

Such problems can never be fully resolved unless a context of assured stability is established: above all, the conditions of insecurity in which local expansionism and exploitation arise as defensive strategies, even when the best intentions prevail, must be eliminated. A larger structure capable of stabilizing the economic setting is necessary, and, if it is to rationalize the economic environment facing each community, it will have to control substantially much wholesale marketing, longer term capital financing, and taxation.

Other issues which cannot be resolved alone by one community point up further functions of a larger framework and a larger decision-making body. These include managing the ecology of a river system, deciding the location of new cities, establishing transportation between population centers, committing capital in large societal investments, and balancing foreign trade.*

Since the socialist argument for a large unit appears to be correct in all these instances, the issues become: How large? And how might it be established without generating a new dynamic toward centralized power? A governing, continental scale "state" would be far too large for any hope of democratic management by localities—and totally unnecessary for technical efficiency save, perhaps, in continental transportation and some forms of power exploitation. (But cooperation *between* areas is feasible, as present international air transport or American tie-ins with Canadian energy sources illustrate.)

Accordingly, once again, as William Appleman Williams and Robert Lafont have suggested, *regional* units organized on the principle of "commonwealth" become significant elements in a solution.** This is the least developed area of

* And, of course, unless such a larger framework is established, it is hard to see how the insecure conditions out of which international expansionism and imperialism grow can be eliminated.

** See William Appleman Williams, *The Great Evasion* (Chicago: Quadrangle Books, 1964); Robert Lafont, *La Revolution Regionaliste* (Paris: Editions Gallimard, 1967). For the idea of regionalism, also see the writings of the American anarchist Alexander Berkman.

theory; however, some intermediate unit larger than a "community" but smaller than a nation of 300 million people appears to be required. For many economic matters the present states are too small, and most lack a tradition of direct economic responsibility. The unit must be capable of taking over directly (and decentralizing!) capital and productive functions now controlled by, say, the 500 largest economic corporations—without escalating to the scale of the entire social system. In America today, though extremely limited in function, the most obvious suggestive example of a regional unit is the Tennessee Valley Authority,* but we should begin to conceive of a system in which this nation, by the end of the century, might be broken into eight or ten confederated regions of 20 to 30 million people, each region made up of confederated communities. Each region might perhaps approximate the scale of the four Scandinavian countries taken together. (New England, Appalachia, Tidelands, Deep South, Midwest, Plains and Mountain States, Southwest, West Coast?) (In Canada, an independent or semi-independent Quebec might be another appropriate regional unit.)

* The T.V.A., of course, is not offered as a "model"—as its failure to resolve many issues (from participation to ecology) warns.

Part of the answer might also involve regional units of different sizes for different purposes. The metropolitan area as a unit, for example, might control certain heavy industries or specialized public services such as intraurban transportation. Some state units might control power development and, building on the state park tradition, could also appropriately manage expanding recreational industries like skiing. A grouping of regions like New England and Appalachia might control electric power production and distribution; the Pacific Coast and the Mountain States might unite for a variety of functions, particularly for rational ecological planning and watershed control. In such instances, organization *across* regions is more rational. Black Americans and other minorities may for political reasons also wish to establish racially organized associations *across the nation*. The point of regional organization as a guideline is not to exclude collaboration but rather to attempt to solve some problems of cooperation and power by building up units of rational scale which are still manageable by the localities implicit in a decentralist vision. . . .

PLANNING, POWER, AND PROCESS

Within the larger unit decisions should reflect

the needs of real (that is to say, local) communities. But to avoid wastes and inequalities, higher-order planning is obviously also necessary. The issues then are: Who controls the planners? And how are fundamental planning criteria determined? The thrust of the argument is that controlling criteria should in part be generated out of expressed community needs and experiences, out of specific demands for goods and services—over time, through stages—*and* that these must be bolstered by the development of independent local bases of power. At all levels, the appropriate units' control of a local market through its direct receipt of some surpluses and its control of some capital, can offer economic leverage, just as its organization principles permit political leverage. The larger unit must have sufficient autonomous power, however, to balance the pressures from the strongest communities (but not so much as to overwhelm them). . . .

In general, the difficult broader principle in a three-level vision of cooperative community, economic region, and confederated nation is to anchor units in new social structures which preserve sufficient independence of decision and power (without which neither freedom nor responsibility is possible), but which are not so powerful as to produce unrestrained competition and deny the possibility of a substantial measure of rational planning. . . . The rule should be to leave as many functions as possible to localities, elevating only what is absolutely essential to the higher unit. . . .

A critical problem is to <u>define *specific* ways in which people living in localities</u> might <u>con-strain larger-order systems without making it impossible for them to function</u>. Here, some clues are available from modern American ex-perience: in the Tennessee Valley Authority, for instance, local corporation farms (and other pri-vate business interests), rather than "communi-ties," to a great extent keep the bureaucrats in line, serving *their* purposes—but T.V.A. author-ities still retain sufficient power rationally to control much river development.*

What if *communities* were the power base or building blocks of a new political-economy? They might reduce regional units to more lim-ited roles, largely responsible to (in part "co-

---

* The way military contractors and the various ser-vices often *partially* "co-opt" the Federal civilian de-fense bureaucracy, paralleling the corporation farms of the T.V.A., is also instructive. Only in imagination do Defense Department bureaucrats simply "order" the corporations, the services, and their Congressional allies to do their bidding. In fact, the reverse is closer to a description of a reality which involves a complex interaction of centralized bureaucratic direction and sub-unit lobbying and pressure.

opted" by) the interests of the people—organized in new cooperative community forms.
Given the proper social basis, a large unit like a
region might be kept in check. Its ultimate role
would then be partly simply coordination; its
broad policy-making and administrative functions would depend upon the development (and
acceptance) of a rationally articulated political
program. A two-chamber legislature might perhaps represent the organized communities, on
the one hand, and the interests of the people at
large, on the other. . . .

In this setting, several other basic questions
could be addressed: what, for example, might
be the best process for making decisions over
such fundamental issues as *how* population
should be dispersed; *whether* to make major new
society-shaping investments, as in one or another transportation system; *how much* should
be allocated to prevent the destruction of the
environment (directly, or indirectly through the
greater allocation of time entailed by some—but
not all—voluntaristic methods); *how much* of
society's resources to allocate between consumption and investment (which also entails many
ecological considerations, including the question
of a zero growth rate).

"Planning" is obviously required here too,
but again it is important to recognize that in this

sketch of an alternative program, the process of central "planning" would be quite different from that of the rationalized state or the Soviet "command economy." It would be much more organic: social priorities would be developed through local processes in each community, and then "integrated" subsequently through regional and national politics generated out of local experience. Ultimately, the central regional and national bodies would have to resolve conflicting claims about resource allocation through the more broadly representative political processes. . . .

To identify socialism with streamlined, computerized planning, as some do, is a fatal error. "Planning" would more likely be an "iterative" phenomenon involving: first, information, priorities and criteria generated at local levels; next an integration at a higher order "planning stage"; then the implications calculated; a return to smaller units for reconsideration; and finally back up again. (The Chinese call a similar process "two ups and two downs"; and some large U.S. corporations have developed sophisticated linear programming models for their decentralized internal management which are of relevance.)

One must recognize that decentralized, democratic planning inevitably involves inefficiencies and considerably more time. However, if successful, the gains in released energies, to say nothing of the quality of life, are likely to more than compensate for what is lost. . . .

But this returns us to the question of whether the basic social units in which day-to-day life occur are, in fact, likely to sustain new, more humane experiences of community. It should again be clear why it is important to place priority on local social structures and processes which have a potential for developing and prefiguring a new ethic of cooperation, even if this may mean local communities initially function to an extent competitively as market operators. Staging is critical: could social relationships within communities be strengthened so as to alter values and modify external relations *over time?* Could a cooperative development process permit the *subsequent* establishment of the necessary coordinating structures between communities and, in combination with national political efforts, the larger framework for the overall economy?

There are no easy answers to such questions and very little guidance available from foreign experience or past history. Chinese and Israeli developments suggest that communities may be able to sustain and deepen the quality of internal social relations at the same time external relations involve both the limited use of market competition and a larger framework. Marxist theoreticians as different as Charles Bettelheim and Paul Sweezy agree, too, that the use *both* of a limited competitive market *and* planning seem inevitable at certain stages of development under all forms of socialism. . . .* Competition can then be viewed not as a method of exploitation but as a tool of rational administration. One challenge, it accordingly appears, is to be able to recognize the latter and eliminate the former, and (if the social system is to overcome its origins in capitalism), to attempt shrewd trade-offs between competition and cooperation *at different stages of development,* as a new experiential basis emerges, as mutual needs develop, as larger national political possibilities open up, and as a new vision is created. . . .

In such a long process of development, as Martin Buber urged, the permissive environment which may be attainable if localities are not totally subservient to central agencies is more important, initially, than the apparent top-down

---

* See, for instance, their exchange in *Monthly Review,* Vol. 22, No. 7 (December 1970), pp. 1–21. For an introduction to Chinese practices, see John G. Gurley, "Capitalist and Maoist Economic Development," *Monthly Review,* Vol. 22, No. 9 (February 1971).

rationality of centralized planning systems. The conservative, the Yugoslav, the Israeli, the Chinese, and the anarchist all seem right also to argue that a degree of local autonomy and a degree of competition must be assured if freedom and spontaneous innovation are to continue over time. . . .

EQUALITY?

One issue noted in passing deserves special consideration: equality. Grant that communities might develop new cooperative ways, grant they might begin to develop a different ethic, a different concept of the nature of community and cooperation, grant even that they might help each other to a greater extent than under capitalism, there is, nonetheless, no obvious reason why rich communities should be expected in practice to share their wealth with other communities. (In Yugoslavia, there are still regions of the nation in which workers earn one-fifth as much for the same work as in wealthier regions!) Globally, one need only compare the living standards of various socialist countries to be reminded that even when the rhetoric of equality is proclaimed, new social structures (in this case involving whole nations) do not automatically achieve it in practice.

There are, I think, two answers to the dilemma of equality: first (and this is crucial), America is so far advanced technologically that with different organization, it ultimately would not be a great burden to pull lagging areas of the nation up. The society is not a Yugoslavia fighting to climb the steep hill of capital accumulation. Even now, at the top of the system, young people are falling away from the false affluence of consumerism. Were the waste of unemployment, militarism, and unnecessary consumption ended, the resources available would be enormous. Poor communities could be aided without intolerable cost. It would also be possible to allocate huge resources to other nations.

Second, politics would not die were the nation organized as a many-level Pluralist Commonwealth. (Indeed, what we are talking about might best be defined not as an *achieved,* static goal, but as a stage-by-stage *process* of increasing mastery of rational and irrational limitations on man's potential.) Even today, politics forces the creeping federal structure to reallocate funds in some programs, though it does so very erratically. In a new Commonwealth, local and regional bodies would have substantial influence on major decisions of investment and resource allocation which are now left to private corporations. Especially as a new vision and ethic develops, it is possible to imagine a considerably reinvigorated politics which could concentrate on helping underdeveloped communities—perhaps progressively narrowing the range of inequality by setting (and gradually lowering) maximum income ceilings, by setting (and gradually raising) minimum income floors, and by regularly introducing a greater share of such free goods as education, medical care, housing, and basic food stuffs.*

But a progressive process of this kind is not the same as total equality, and the distinction should make it clear that a fundamental point is at issue. The only alternative to the process of politics is a central decision-making authority which *forces* its program upon all communities. *You simply cannot have it both ways.* A basic problem of both democracy and equality is when

---

* Over a specified period—say, 25 years—it might be possible to achieve complete equality, perhaps through raising minimum income levels by say, 3 percent per annum—and progressively lowering the ceiling on incomes through taxation and other means by another 1 percent per annum. For a discussion of related issues, see Howard J. Sherman, "The Economics of Pure Communism," *The Review of Radical Political Economics,* Volume II, Number 4 (Winter 1970); and Frank Roosevelt, "Market Socialism: A Humane Economy?", *Journal of Economic Issues,* Vol. V, No. 2 (April 1971), and his exchange with M. Bronfenbrenner, in the subsequent June 1971 issue.

and what is to be centralized and what is not—and at which stages of development very specific trade-offs between conflicting values are to be made. There is an obvious trade-off at one level of theory between equality and decentralization; place absolute priority on the former and you must have enormous power at the center to end variations between localities. On the other hand, if diversity and democracy are priorities, they bring with them a substantial degree of inequality between areas.

Other considerations make it appear that the nature of the trade-offs is even more complex. Although centralization in theory can establish equality *between areas*, historically, simply to function, most hierarchical systems have required highly stratified, unequal patterns of *individual incentives*. (The resulting inequality of state-socialist systems in practice is often ignored by their proponents and apologists.) Motivation is potentially quite different, however, in small units (like the kibbutz) in which almost the only historic examples of substantial equality *between* individuals are known. But at the outset, semi-autonomous small-unit development inevitably means inequality *between areas*. Therefore, while centralization seems the short cut to equality, it is likely in practice to be a dead end. And while diversity and democracy seem to be antagonistic to equality, this appears to be the only way to build up different motivational patterns out of which an ethic of universal equality might eventually develop.*

For this reason, too—and because voluntary, individual choice is critical to the development of a new ethic—a "second tier" to the economy might also be appropriate: Paul and Percival Goodman (and Arthur Waskow) have suggested that individuals be free to largely opt out of the overall economy, if they so choose, and that they be guaranteed a minimum subsistence income much less than the basic economy's norm.** They could then choose freely whether or not to accept the more stringent disciplines (and greater material benefits of the larger system. One imagines a society open enough to appreciate people moving back and forth between the two tiers—like commune youths working at the

---

* Space limitations preclude a full discussion of international issues, but the above observations may also help suggest a *general* perspective on long term trade-offs and stages to consider in connection with resource reallocations not only between rich and poor communities, but between rich and poor *nations* as well.

** The Goodmans reckon that a reasonable "subsistence" level could be maintained by allocating one tenth to one fifteenth of society's production: Hence "necessary labor" would be very minimal. Waskow suggests a subsistence income should, in any event, be one half the average. See Goodman and Goodman, op. cit., p. 191, and Arthur Waskow, "The 1990 Draft Constitution," *Motive,* March 1971.

post office when monetary needs arise or when making the transitions that real psychological growth requires . . .

The fundamental (and difficult) point is that complex trade-offs and stages of development are inevitable; the issue is whether wise balances between divergent objectives can be struck continuously at different points as the historic process moves forward. Once again there are no simple, "either/or" answers. . . .

Over the long haul the trade-offs between centralization and decentralization are likely to diminish as increasingly productive technology makes it easier to satisfy more needs—and as rational ecological judgments reduce the pressure for economic growth. If individual and community motivation for exorbitant living standards can be reduced there will also be less need for the hierarchical and centralized controls that ever-expanding production seems to require. Finally, as true (and voluntary) *agreement with* the principles of a new vision of equality develops, centralized decision-making to achieve it can, in fact, become more a matter of rational co-ordination and administration than of bureaucratic compulsion.

In the final analysis, therefore, the tension between the socialist vision and decentralist alternatives may perhaps best be understood not as an ultimate contradiction but as a transitional problem of societies moving toward the post-industrial era. . . .

PRECURSORS AND PREFIGURATIONS?

. . . A variety of existing youth communes and collectives point in the direction of small scale cooperative community. Affluent white youths' need to transcend isolated individualism seems to be generated systematically out of the sterility of high income suburban (and nuclear family) life, out of the collectivizing experience of migration to the (university) ghetto, and out of the general contradiction between liberal expectations for fulfillment and American realities. Hesitant and beleaguered though they are, collectives and communes all over the country are experimental arenas in which some cooperative "commonwealth" values are being learned in practice—and in which the outlines of a new social vision are beginning, however falteringly, to emerge. . . .*

Far more significant developments related to the concept of a Pluralist Commonwealth are to

---

* A parallel and supportive experimental trend involves the introduction of sophisticated existential/humanist therapeutic insights into group process—from encounter to "therapeutic communities" to "gestalt kibbutzim" and beyond.

be found in parts of the black community, particularly in a few areas which are politically far ahead of the nation. Increasing numbers of black Americans today are attempting to articulate the idea of "the community" and are beginning to experiment with ways to institutionalize the notion that *its* interests should take priority. Here, the collective ideal and higher expectations seem rooted partly in earlier agrarian traditions, partly in collectivizing migrations to the (urban) ghetto, the experience of rising income levels (as compared with the rural South), and the contradiction between raised hopes and brutal denial and repression. All have been important (and are continuing) conditions out of which a new vision is slowly being forged.

If youth experiments attempt to realize co-operative social values in isolated settings from New Mexico to Vermont, or the permissive but atypical atmosphere of a university town, in most ghettos the notion of "community" has for the most part been expressed as a demand for control of institutions in existing neighborhoods, like Harlem or Hough. The emerging concept of the "community corporation" is taking on increasing importance in this context— and may become a critical element in an "alternative program" if it transcends the limitations of the inevitable initial compromises.

The mechanisms of a democratically controlled neighborhood corporation involve little more than drawing a legal line around a neighborhood or rural area to establish a geographically defined corporate entity which may undertake a variety of social, economic, and political functions. The crucial feature is democracy—either through the principle of one person, one vote; or through confederations of local block clubs, churches, and action organizations.

Though sometimes conceived only as O.E.O. vehicles or instruments of "neighborhood government," such institutions become of much greater long-run interest when they assume ownership of industries and stores collectively in the name of the entire community, as they are now doing in many areas. The terms "community union," "community cooperative," or "community development corporation" (C.D.C.) are then more accurate descriptions. Instead of letting individual capitalists buy businesses and absorb the profits themselves, a C.D.C. either distributes small dividends to all members or, more significantly, it uses proceeds collectively for such community-building services as day care centers, recreational programs, or training activities.

Some C.D.C.'s (like FIGHT, in Rochester,

New York) are already operating community-owned electrical manufacturing plants of substantial scale. In Los Angeles, Operation Bootstrap has established a cooperatively owned toy factory; in the Chicano community of New Mexico there are a variety of cooperatively owned industries ranging from farming and cattle feeding to furniture and wood products manufacturing; in Cleveland, a rubber molding factory is collectively owned; in Philadelphia there is already a large community-owned shopping center (and one which is to be more broadly based in the community is in the planning stages in Cleveland). . . .*

In one or two instances, particularly in the New Communities, Inc. experiment in southwest Georgia, the vision of community has been developed much further, and has led to the purchase of land for a black, collectively owned city based on communitarian ideals—similar in hope, if not yet in practice, to the Israeli *moshav*. Obviously, none of the experiments represents the achievement of a fully developed alternative vision; their significance is only as possible "precursors" and "prefigurations" in a long process

* For information on these and other efforts, write to the Center for Community Economic Development, 1878 Massachusetts Avenue, Cambridge, Massachusetts 02140.

which might conceivably transcend what must begin as "community capitalism". . . .

Two distinct ways of organizing power to bolster these community efforts have emerged: in many cities demonstrations, sit-ins, and other militant protests have successfully wrenched control of housing and even urban renewal from public bureaucracy—and placed ownership and control in the hands of community groups. Elsewhere, a more traditional form of power which attaches to the voting strength of well-organized groups has forced many concessions. In New Mexico, for instance, at one point state authorities were brought to direct state schools and hospitals to give preferential treatment to the purchase of vegetables from local community cooperatives.

The linkage between a local, community-owned vegetable cooperative and a higher-order political authority is of special interest in that it illustrates in skeletal outline what might be thought of as a two-tier Pluralist Commonwealth model. In this instance, the local community-based economic effort is fortified by political-economic decisions made by the higher unit—however, given the power relationships, it is forced to be responsive to a coalition of smaller scale units. The relationship of the mayor to community groups in Cleveland, Ohio, suggests similar possibilities may emerge elsewhere (and pressure for preferential Federal purchasing is already developing). . . .

Community corporations are only one illustration of the general concept of community-wide efforts: the program of the Calumet Community Congress in Gary, Indiana, and the tax and municipal power programs of radicals elected to the city council in Berkeley, California, might help open the way for similar developments in white communities. So might the spontaneously developed municipal ownership schemes which Rockville, Maryland, officials have instituted to help resolve their local fiscal problems. There are also interesting community-based economic experiments underway in Appalachia and some ethnic communities of the Boston, Massachusetts, area. (Related to all of this is a point of great political potential which could be exploited by radicals: University of California researchers have recently shown that local taxes could be greatly reduced if new town development—on new land or as the *reconstruction* of old neighborhoods—is owned by a non-profit corporation so that profits flow directly to the local community. . . .) But these forms and ideas are only preliminaries: the development of appropriate, high-technology, and authentically American community institutions will have to build on, but greatly transcend, initial experiments and conceptions. . . .

Hannah Arendt has urged that we give renewed attention to the history of the "council" movement—the spontaneous eruption in history of *local,* people's governing bodies. The contemporary trend toward community control is, in fact, best understood as part of a tradition which includes Jefferson's idea of "ward republics," and extends through the Paris Commune, the *soviets,* the Mexican *ejida,* the Algerian *autogestion* system, etc.* Though not the result of national upheaval, some of the new American institutions, moreover, emphasize explicitly (as did not all the previous institutions) the socialist concept of direct (local) common ownership of property. That community-owned efforts are at this stage only fragmentary and partial is obvious; their importance may be more as educative vehicles which teach basic concepts related to the vision of a Pluralist Commonwealth than

---

* See her *On Revolution* (New York: Viking Press, 1963). That the historic movements largely failed is reason to consider carefully not only their great importance, but what must be added to the tradition to make it relevant and viable in the specific conditions of our own technological development and historical period. And it is reason to confront the need to develop a new awareness, specific ideas, and a commitment based on understanding of what it will take to offset the enormous modern pressures toward centralization.

as ultimate structures. The question is whether the social and economic forms that are suggested can be extended (and combined with the development of regional and national alternatives) in the longer struggle to build new political power. . . .*

* Such a political effort, in my opinion, will do well to avoid sterile "either/or" rhetorical debates by combining in new ways neighborhood *and* workplace organizing, tax resistance *and* demands for better community service, tactics involving confrontation *and* prefiguratory counter-institutions, local, regional *and* national actions and alliances, etc. Discussion of the appropriate mixes, strategies, and timing of such a long-term politics will be taken up in a forthcoming publication.

ADDENDA TO THE "NOTES"

BY GAR ALPEROVITZ

This sketch of some criteria for strategy and program is included partly to suggest the place of positive program in a longer term overview, partly to clarify some areas of commonality (and difference) between Staughton Lynd's essay and my own. As will be evident, the specific elements here integrated are drawn from the activist and intellectual work of countless people in whose debt we all stand (which is only another way to say that all knowledge is social). I am only too aware of the difficulty (and advantage?) that a preliminary attempt at generalized integration, abstracted as it is from its larger context, may raise as many questions as it resolves.

. . . These elements may be offered as a potential framework for discussion of the relationship between strategy and program:

Immediate reforming demands which can achieve small victories (and real improvements), illuminate tensions inherent in the political-economy, and—if linked with an explicit strategy—help suggest the limits of the present system and the need for a fundamental transformation:

I. Specific organizing efforts including neighborhood confrontation, municipal electoral campaigns, referenda, etc., to secure popular *local control over*—and *redirection of*—a variety of such public programs as: education, medical care, urban renewal, rent control, public housing, transportation, etc.;

II. Specific efforts, including both direct action and political organizing, to obtain positive local, state, and national legislation to *expand resources* in such programs (and in adequate income maintenance programs)—as a matter of right;

III. Broader *national* efforts to *end the war* and other military, political, and economic interventions, *reduce military spending,* and *shift resources* to programs structured along the above lines so far as possible;

IV. *Simultaneously:* organizing efforts by public employees (teachers, sanitation workers, administrators, etc.) to secure equitable *higher wages* and *more public service jobs* under worker/community control—demands which may both bring immediate gains, and, again, increase pressure for a redirection of state resources to legitimate purposes;

All of the above combined with efforts to tap that huge share of society's income and wealth now controlled by elites and corporations —in order to benefit the vast majority, illuminate inequities, and explicate contradictions of the present system, and help pose the fundamental issue of what could be achieved if society's income and wealth benefited the entire community directly.

V. *Simultaneously:* specific programs to *reduce* or *end taxation* not only for the "poor" but progressively for a *majority* of citizens, up to incomes in the $12,000–$15,000 range— again, demands designed to obtain specific gains, and, strategically, to increase awareness that a major restructuring of state finance is necessary. Especially, an end to sales taxes, property taxes on housing, and social security levies;

VI. *Simultaneously:* efforts (activist, political, legislative) to *shift the tax burden onto the elite* (minority) top 15–20 percent of the income pyramid, with steeply progressive taxation above $20,000—*and, onto the major corporations.*

Especially heavy taxation of dividends, rents, profits, inheritances, and other unearned receipts derived solely from title to property; a sharpening of the distinction between "earned" and "unearned" income.

The uniting of both taxpayer's organizations *and* public employees (e.g. teachers) in common efforts: lower taxes for the majority *and* better pay—made possible through taxation of the elites and corporations, and, ultimately, through community ownership of revenue-producing enterprise (housing and development corporations, land trusts, municipal power, etc.);

VII. The latter efforts accompanied by a

strategy *to constrain private corporate control of economic surpluses*—including programs (and coordinated national organizing) to prevent corporations from shifting wage increases and taxes to the consumer through higher prices: price controls, *not* wage controls, except above $15,000–$20,000.

Especially efforts to exploit local opportunities for community control of prices (rents) in tenant-occupied housing—again, both to secure specific improvements in geographically defined organizing areas and to apply pressure against exploitative private landlords; *simultaneously,* development of parallel cooperative and community owned housing to illustrate a structural alternative to private property. Similarly: efforts to strengthen control of gas and electric prices *combined with* parallel development of cooperative or municipally owned utilities. The same strategy applied ultimately to all significant productive enterprise—locally, regionally, nationally;

VIII. Strikes and other actions by working Americans (blue and white collar) to secure higher minimum wage laws, *higher wages* for those below $12,000–$15,000, and *control over working conditions*—all (together with demands for price controls and increased taxation) to help set limits on corporate control of economic surpluses.

Actions also to constrain corporate investment abroad—both to halt interventionism and to underscore how such (and other) private investment decisions contribute to domestic unemployment and other irrationalities;

The above efforts—which in part coincide with a "New Populism"—combined with long range educational programs to suggest the inherent limitations of movements which (despite positive intent) do not confront the basic power realities; hence, the need ultimately for a fundamentally different economic system—one which, as a matter of structural principle, does not (as now) permit the elite top 20 percent regularly to garner 40–46 percent of society's income (leaving the 80 percent majority make do on what is left); which does not permit less than 2 percent to own 80 percent of the corporate stock held personally, 90 percent of the corporate bonds, virtually 100 percent of state and local bonds; which does not permit concentrated private corporate control of society's main productive wealth by 200–500 giant firms, etc.

IX. *Simultaneously,* therefore: all of the

above coupled with activities which seek public *control* over a variety of irresponsible *corporate practices*—from Ralph Nader's limited (but at this stage attention-focusing) demands for responsible production and tougher regulation, to specific ecology, urban, and other anti-corporate direct-action campaigns.

But, also, education to suggest the demonstrable limitations of such approaches (despite their intent); hence, again, the need to establish a dialogue which moves progressively beyond them (even as their immediate educative value is acknowledged) to more fundamental alternatives;

X. Broader national efforts demanding *jobs* (and meaningful work) and an *end to inflation*—coupled with long term educative efforts to increase understanding that a corporately-organized, profit-motivated economic system is substantially incapable of fulfilling such demands; that, accordingly, a new publicly responsible system is needed.

Efforts to establish preliminary positive experiments which illustrate a basic structural alternative, slowly prefigure the elements of a new society, and, over the long haul, tie in with attempts to mobilize an effective new social movement and political alliance rooted in the vast majority:

XI. All of the above accompanied by the buildup over time of *alternative institutions* capable of meeting immediate needs (free schools, clinics, day care, etc.)—especially institutions which, through cooperative community control of productive capital *and* public services, begin to suggest economic principles and structures related to a society-wide commonwealth vision.

Cooperatives, community development corporations, various municipal ownership efforts, and cooperative housing major priorities —above all those which use some surpluses directly and illustratively (in contrast to taxes on the majority) to provide some community services.

But also, communes, small group encounter, and self-transformation efforts which teach voluntary cooperation, a sense of community, and, generally, awareness of one's personal responsibility for the existential, social, political, and economic consequences of one's actions (or inactions);

Special efforts—as in attempts to establish radically *new communities*—to offer paradigmatic demonstrations of how an *integrated* vision of a new community (implicit in the ideal of a new society) might actually function in practice (Southwest Georgia, New Communities, Inc., an important beginning effort; Cambridge Institute New City Prospectus, a suggestive initial sketch);

XII. *Political and legislative efforts to support various positive experimental programs* through grants, long term loans, "vouchers," technical assistance, favored tax treatment;

XIII. All of the above accompanied by an attempt to mobilize a new *cross-cultural majoritarian alliance approached from two intersecting directions:*
Efforts to organize around demands which sharpen the distinction between the majority of taxpayers, on the one hand, and the elites and corporations which control the bulk of income and wealth, on the other;
Efforts to build positive *parallel alternative institutions* in *both* the black and white geographic neighborhoods of the same constituency—and alliances based on common interest in programs to support such institutions;

XIV. Specific attempts to bring together subgroupings of such alliances within the geographically defined area of the *region*—in political organizing around parallel demands in education, housing, medical care, welfare, and other matters (The Northeast Model Cities Citizens' Union in New England an illustration); in common regional cooperative marketing arrangements; in demands for public regional control of ecological issues (especially river systems), land use, transportation, energy (electric power and gas and oil pricing), and (ultimately) large scale productive industry (Appalachia, a strategic area for developing new regional models);

XV. All of the above linked to a continuing attempt to describe with much greater precision than is now possible *a detailed, rational, coherent idea of what the institutions of a better society—related to the above elements in communities and in regions—would really entail for ordinary people.*

. . . This framework rests on the belief that in the specific conditions of late twentieth-century American capitalism, despite the obvious barriers to change, a new approach is both necessary and possible. Notwithstanding the many failures of modern social movements—and the resulting pessimism—the sixties should at the very least have taught us to question fashionable predictions that nothing can ever change . . . It is important at the very outset to reaffirm the legitimacy of self-evident human needs, and the legitimacy, too, of demanding a society which can meet them. In each instance, therefore, rhetoric must give way to clearly defined program. The relationship between some radical-militant activities *and* some liberal approaches *and* even (as in tax and decentralization issues) some traditionally conservative efforts must be clearly articulated. The broader near-term objectives are to bring people together around common interests, to achieve specific improvements, to raise public consciousness of the limits of the present system, to narrow the power range of corporate institutions, to illuminate the need for fundamental change, and to begin to suggest the specific content of a basic alternative.

The fifteen points here outlined also involve the judgment that as the brief remaining decades of the century are traversed new alliances with various groups, now not often regarded as possible, may well be practical—*if* issues are formulated with a view both to immediate problems and to the logic of the long-term dilemmas facing the American system. This is especially true in the case of demands which link the taxpayer rebellion (and the interests of perhaps 75–80 percent of society) to demands for *expanded* social services in a way which focuses attention on elite and corporate ownership and control of productive wealth. (In a society in which the Net National Product for families of four is near $20,000, both a reduction in taxes for the vast majority and an expansion of services would already be possible were the system rationally restructured—a reality which should become increasingly evident as the contradiction between what is technically feasible and what exists is deepened and clarified over time.) An approach which stresses uniting the "excluded majority" in a variety of complementary ways, moreover, avoids the obstacles standing in the way of reforms which pose the interests of the *bottom* 11–20 percent (black, poor) minority against the interests of the rest of the population, or which stress conflicts between various exploited groups over scarce jobs. An emphasis on the inequities of *the system* may help overcome black/white polarization by defining common organizing targets; and it could complement other attempts to specify parallel black and white *community-based* efforts (medical, economic, housing, highway, etc.) which permit the same redefinition of the common interests of the majority. . . .

In such a broad-scale and long-term effort it is obviously essential to clarify the linkages between political efforts and experimental attempts to erect prefiguratory counter-institutions related to the larger conception of a better society. Implicit, therefore, is the requirement that radicals undertake a self-conscious intellectual effort to sketch a vision of such a society in explainable, common-sense terms—a vision which must inevitably begin as utopian, but which (if it continually incorporates new experience and thought) might ultimately hope to answer that so-legitimate question: What, specifically, do you want?

A Note on the Authors

Staughton Lynd was chairman of the first march against the Vietnam War in Washington, D.C., on April 17, 1965, and director of freedom schools during the Mississippi Summer Project of 1964. An historian, he is currently doing labor history and community organizing in the Calumet area of South Chicago and northern Indiana.

Gar Alperovitz, Fellow of the Institute for Policy Studies, Washington, D.C., and Co-Director of the Cambridge Institute, Cambridge, Massachusetts, is the author of *Atomic Diplomacy: Hiroshima and Potsdam* and *Cold War Essays*.

Beacon Paperback   459 — Political Science

STRATEGY AND PROGRAM

TWO ESSAYS TOWARD A NEW AMERICAN SOCIALISM

by Staughton Lynd and Gar Alperovitz

I s it possible to oppose and change the juggernaut of American decisionmaking processes? Can society be organized in a different way, a more cooperative, more humane way? Staughton Lynd and Gar Alperovitz, scholars and activists, suggest what can be done now and offer important models for a better, more rational world.

Lynd surveys the experiences and differences of the old left and the new left, and offers a concrete discussion of the possible roles of the left in a mass organization. He then presents models for leadership and decisionmaking in a radical mass movement.

Alperovitz provides a model of a pluralist commonwealth with particular emphasis on the control of economic resources and power. In a striking appendix to his essay, he offers fifteen specific proposals, which, if taken up by a broad-based movement, he believes could bring tangible gains, illuminate tensions inherent in larger contradictions emerging in society, suggest the limits of the present system, and help establish a setting for long term fundamental change.

Staughton Lynd, a historian, has in recent years devoted much of his time to community organizing. His most recent book is *The Resistance* with Michael Ferber. Gar Alperovitz, the author of *Atomic Diplomacy: Hiroshima and Potsdam* and *Cold War Essays*, is a Fellow of the Institute for Policy Studies and Co-Director of the Cambridge Institute.

BEACON PRESS   *BOSTON*

ISBN 0–8070–4383–4